icons

Mary Jo Martin, RSHM

Anne White

Ann Brook

Paul Gray

Yvonne May

Damian Walmsley

LIVING
a national project of catechesis & religious education
Sharing OUR FAITH
Catholic Bishops' Conference of England & Wales

Published by HarperCollins*Publishers* Ltd
77–85 Fulham Palace Road
London W6 8JB

© Department for Catholic Education and Formation, Bishops' Conference of England and Wales

www.**Collins**Educational.com
On-line support for schools and colleges

First published 2001

ISBN 0 00 322132 6

Nihil Obstat Fr Anton Cowan, *censor*

Imprimatur Mgr Thomas Egan, V.G.
Westminster, 29th June 2000

The Nihil obstat and Imprimatur are a declaration that a book or pamphlet is considered to be free from doctrinal or moral error. It has not implied that those who have granted the Nihil obstat and imprimatur agree with the contents, opinions or statements expressed.

British Library Cataloguing in Publication Data
A catalogue record for this book is available from the British Library

Project management by Terry Vittachi

Picture research by Kathy Lockley

Design and layout by Ken Vail Graphic Design, Cambridge

Cover design by Ken Vail Graphic Design, Cambridge

Cover photograph
1. Christie's Images Ltd
2. Getty Images

Printed and bound by Scotprint, Haddington, Scotland

Illustrations
Tony Forbes, pp. 21, 32, 36, 72, 76, 85, 92; Rosamund Fowler, pp. 30, 53, 83, 93; Alyson MacNeill, pp. 8, 16, 34, 69, 73, 74, 91; Sally Taylor, pp. 11, 27, 50, 52, 68, 79, 89, 94.

Photographs
A & B News, monthly paper of the Diocese of Arundel & Brighton pp.81, 86; AKG London pp.18, 23, 23, 45, 60, 95/Erich Lessing pp.10, 58/Hilbich p.39/Orsi Battaglini p.23; Ancient Art & Architecture Collection p.16; Andes Press Agency/Carlos Reyes pp.28, 29, 29, 46, 47, 51, 55, 77, 81, 88/Val Baker p.6; Art Directors & TRIP Photo Library/A.Tovy p.62/B.Turner p.43/D.Houghton p.43/Dinodia p.49/G.Turner p.21/Helene Rogers pp.15, 16, 26, 26, 43, 56, 57/M.Keep p.7/S.Grant pp.35, 57; Bridgeman Art Library London/Vatican Museums & Galleries, Vatican City, Italy p.22; CNS Photos, Washington DC p.20; © CORBIS p.77; Mary Evans Picture Library p.18C/Sarah Lorimer Collection p.19; Fotomas Index (UK) p.17; Robert Harding Picture Library pp.21, 21, 38, 43, 54, 55, 55, 57, 62, 70; © HarperCollins Publishers pp.39, 42, 64; HCPT – The Pilgrimage Trust p.7; Hulton Getty/Auerbach p.38; Courtesy of the Kairos Centre pp.12, 28, 90; © Sieger Koder: Fusswaschung p.44; Courtesy of Terry & Brian Lawton p.84; © 1978, MISEREOR Medienproduktion, Aachen, Germany p.41; Novosti (London) p.15; 'PA' Photos p.37/Neil Munns p.35; Panos Pictures/Jean-Léo Dugast p.38/Andrew Testa p.49; Photofusion/Bob Watkins p.78/David Tothill p.47/Paul Baldesare p.59; Courtesy of Phular Studios, Alfreton Rd., Nottingham p.80; Private Collection p.30; Rex Features pp.6, 12, 19, 19, 35, 46, 62, 62, 88/Brendan/Beirne p.55/Brian Lawrence p.9/Simon Roberts p.6/SIPA pp.37, 77; Courtesy of the De la Salle Brothers p.90; Courtesy of The Samaritans p.35; Still Pictures/Denis Bringard p.15/Klein/Hubert p.15; © Benedictine Sisters of Turvey Abbey published by McCrimmon Publishing Company Ltd p.65; Photo Viron, Lourdes p.81; Courtesy of the Diocese of Wrexham p.81

Text
The publishers gratefully acknowledge the following for permission to reproduce copyright material. Every effort has been made to contact the holders of copyright material, but if any have been inadvertently overlooked, the publishers will be pleased to make the necessary arrangements at the first opportunity.

p. 9, extract from *To be a Pilgrim* by Basil Hume, published by St. Paul's; reprinted with permission of St Paul's Publishing; extract from 'The Commentary on Psalm 1' is taken from *The Hidden Fountain*, edited by Thomas Spidlik, published by New City; reprinted with permission; p. 13, 'Oh God, you search me and you know me', © Bernadette Farrell; p. 21, 'The Leader' by Roger McGough, from *Poems on the Underground*; © Roger McGough, reprinted with permission of Peters Fraser & Dunlop Group Limited on behalf of Roger McGough; p. 25, extract from 'Here I am, Lord', © 1981 Daniel L Schutte and New Dawn Music, 5536 NE Hassalo, Portland, OR 97213; all rights reserved; used with permission; p. 38, extract from 'The Road Not Taken' from *The Poetry of Robert Frost*, edited by Edward Connery Lathem, the Estate of Robert Frost and Jonathan Cape as publisher; used by permission of The Random House Group Limited; p. 42, Extract from *The Door Wherein I Went* by Lord Hailsham, published by HarperCollins Publishers; used with permission; extract from 'The Servant King' by Graham Kendrick, © 1983 Kingsway's Thankyou Music; p. 48, 'Love is His word' by Luke Connaughton, © McCrimmon Publishing Company Limited; used with permission; pp. 52–4, excerpts from the English translation of *The Roman Missal*, © 1973, International Committee on English in the Liturgy, Inc (ICEL); all rights reserved; reprinted with permission; p. 56, 'This is my body' by Jimmy Owens; © 1978 Bud John Songs/EMI Christian Music Publishing/CopyCare, PO Box 77, Hailsham BN27 3EF, UK music@copycare.com; reprinted with permission; p. 64, extract from 'Jubilee Song' © 1999, Bernadette Farrell, published by OCP Publications, 5536 NE Hassalo, Portland, OR 97213; all rights reserved; used with permission; p. 66, 'One More Step' by Sydney Carter; reprinted with permission of Stainer & Bell Limited; p. 82, extract from 'Enemy of Apathy' (Wild Goose Publications, 1988), words & music by John L Bell and Graham Maule; © 1988 WGRG, Iona Community, 840 Govan Road, Glasgow G51 3UU, Scotland; reprinted with permission; p. 88, extract from 'Brother, let me be your servant, The Servant Song' by Richard Gillard; © 1977 Scripture in Song, a division of Integrity Music/Adm; by Kingsway's Thankyou Music, P O Box 75, Eastbourne, East Sussex BN23 6NW, UK; for the territory of the UK; used by permission; p.93, extract from 'Kingdom Vision' by Archbishop Oscar Romero, El Salvador, Central America; p. 96, 'O Lord, all the world belongs to you' by Patrick Appleford, © Josef Weinberger Limited, London; reproduced with permission; scriptures quoted from *The Good News Bible* published by The Bible Societies/HarperCollins Publishers Limited, UK © American Bible Society, 1966, 1971, 1976, 1992.

Foreword

On behalf of the Bishops' Conference, I am very pleased to welcome the publication of *Icons*.

Diocesan RE advisers, teachers and many others from all the dioceses of England and Wales have worked extremely hard in the production of this programme, which forms an important part of the National Project. I thank them for their dedication and perseverance.

At the Low Week 2000 Meeting of the Bishops' Conference of England and Wales, the bishops published a statement on Religious Education in Catholic Schools. In it they said that the primary purpose of classroom religious education in a Catholic school is:

'To draw pupils into a systematic study of the teaching of the Church, the saving mystery of Christ which the Church proclaims.' (para 7)

In undertaking this task, schools will benefit greatly from the provision of good teaching resources. For this reason I welcome *Icons*, for it will help Catholic schools to fulfil these expectations during the critical years of Key Stage Three.

In their statement, the bishops also stated:

'The importance of the teacher of RE cannot be exaggerated. We are most grateful to all those teachers who, week in and week out, have contributed to the religious education of pupils in our schools … We salute the generosity of the teachers who have brought not only a love of their faith to their teaching but also a deep concern for the well-being of every pupil.' (para 12)

I gladly repeat that thanks and express my own encouragement for teachers in their important task.

Archbishop Vincent Nichols
Chairman
Department for Catholic Education and Formation

6 June 2000

Acknowledgements

Icons is the fruit of a shared vision, commitment and work. It derives its strength from a long and rigorous process of consultation with Bishops, Diocesan RE advisers, teachers and students of all twenty-two dioceses of England and Wales. It is a key component of the Bishops' national project of catechesis and religious education.

Thanks, first of all, to Bishop Edwin Regan, Chairman of the Steering Committee of the National Project, for his leadership and commitment, and to the members of that Committee: Mr Anthony Clark, Canon Peter Humfrey, Sr Victoria Hummell, Rev Liam Kelly, Mrs Oona Stannard and Rev George Stokes.

Thanks to the Bishops' Conference, and in particular to Archbishops Patrick Kelly and Vincent Nichols, Bishops Daniel Mullins, Edwin Regan and Peter Smith for their time and attention in the final stages of scrutiny.

Since 1996, Diocesan secondary RE advisers and teacher representatives have been actively involved in the development of *Icons*. For their time, energy and expertise, thanks to: Rev Joseph Quigley, Miss Collette Dawson, Rev Ieuan Wyn Jones, Rev Dennis Sutton, Miss Marjorie Parker, Rev Sean Hall, Miss Anne Sales, Miss Sheila O'Brien, Mr Nicholas Weeks, Rev Nigel Bavidge, Rev Des Seddon, Mr Tony Lamb, Sr Aidan Richards, Sr Margaret Horan, Ms Anne-Marie McIntosh, Sr Maura McMenamin, Mr Adrian Dempsey, Mrs Rita Price, Br Charles Gay, Mr Paul Uden, Mr Paul Rowlands, Rev Adrian Morrin, Sr Dolores Lynn, and Ms Noreen O'Neill, secondary advisor of CAFOD. Thanks also to the teachers and students of the schools in every diocese who took part in the monitored trial in 1999 for their support. We hope they will recognise some of their ideas in the final text.

Particular thanks to those who were involved in early stages of development: Mr Tony Castle, Mrs Jane Ranzetta, Mr Simon Danes and to their families and schools: St Bernard's School, Westcliff on Sea, New Hall School, Chelmsford and Cardinal Newman, Hove. Also to Maria Ivko, whose creative contribution remains as a lasting memorial to her dedication to Catholic education. May she rest in peace.

Special thanks to Dr Thomas Allain-Chapman, Commissioning Editor at HarperCollins, with whom the professional aspects of the work became a sharing of ideas that enhanced the development of *Icons*.

To Sisters Mary, Elizabeth and Cecelia and the staff at the Kairos Centre for their hospitality, interest and encouragement and care for our well-being during long working sessions.

To our families and friends we owe tremendous gratitude. They, too, laboured with us through their understanding, patience and listening. Special thanks to Sr Mary Jo's community of the Religious of the Sacred Heart of Mary, and colleagues at St Mary's College, Strawberry Hill, to Anne's colleagues at the Catholic Education Service and to the headteachers, staff and students of St Angela's, Forest Gate, St Bede's, Scunthorpe, St Benedict's, Whitehaven, St Bonaventure's, Forest Gate and St Mary's College, Hull. We could not have completed the task without your support.

Finally, thanks to all those involved in the final stages of production: text editor, picture research, designers, artists and photographers.

The journey has been long. In one sense, with the publication of the text, it has just begun. It has been a tremendous privilege to be part of the creation and development of *Icons*. Our hope is that teachers and students will find here a programme of religious education that enables, illumines and leads to a discovery of the power of faith and the adventure that is the search for meaning and for God.

Mary Jo Martin RSHM, Anne White, Ann Brook, Paul Gray, Yvonne May, Damian Walmsley

Contents

Unit 1   **Faith challenges**   6–36

1A   To be a pilgrim   6–13

1B   Time challenges   14–20

1C   Leadership challenges   21–25

1D   Prayer challenges   26–31

1E   Hope challenges   32–36

Unit 2   **At the heart of belief**   37–66

2A   Word made flesh   37–42

2B   Love   43–48

2C   Sacrifice   49–56

2D   Resurrection   57–61

2/3E   Something worth living for   62–66

Other faiths: Islam   67–70

Unit 3   **A vision for living**   71–96

3A   The common good   71–76

3B   Living powerful lives   77–82

3C   Living commitment   83–88

3D   Living the Gospel   89–96

Pilgrims at the Holy Door, St Peter's, Rome.

Wembley Stadium.

Pilgrims at Mecca.

Pilgrims at Walsingham.

In this section of our work we will be learning:

◆ about what it means to be a pilgrim
◆ about Christian understanding of life as a pilgrimage
◆ how the commandments are a guide for life's pilgrimage.

Paul's story

I was looking forward to the school trip to the war cemeteries of Flanders.

I was also a bit nervous. My mum had told me that my great-grand uncle's grave was there. She said she would get the place and number for me and I could find it. I wasn't sure I wanted to, but I said OK. When we got to the cemetery there were hundreds of graves. Rows and rows and rows of white gravestones. Everything looked clean and the grass was cut. Some graves had flowers and there were some other people around, but it was very quiet. It seemed wrong to talk loudly. Mrs Martin, our teacher, showed the guide the information, and he said he would take us to my great-grand uncle's grave. It's hard to explain how I felt. Mrs Martin asked everyone to give me some time on my own. I looked at the gravestone. 'Paul Forest', it said, same name as me. Then his regiment, and 'Aged 18'. I'll be 18 in two years. I was glad to be on my own. I was glad I had come. It was a special place.

1. Why do people go to these places?
2. What special places do you visit and why?
3. Is there a place that is special for your family? Why?

Discuss

How did Paul feel before the journey?

Why do you think he had mixed feelings about going?

What did he find?

How did he feel?

What do you think the journey meant to him?

Do you think it will have a lasting impact in his life?

Unit 1 Faith challenges

Research

1. Choose one of the following:

◆ war graves pilgrimage

◆ a holy place in this country or abroad

◆ a place of special interest (for example, an historic site like Stonehenge, the birthplace of a famous person, a place of natural beauty or scientific interest).

These questions may help you to collect your information.

Who might go as a pilgrim?

Why? What would their expectations be?

Who would go as a visitor or tourist?

What makes the difference?

2. Present your information as a 'Pilgrim's pack'.

Include:

◆ how to get there (travel details)

◆ what preparations will be needed (tickets, accommodation)

◆ what people will need to take (tent, food)

◆ what would be of interest to a pilgrim, a visitor or tourist

◆ any dos and don'ts

◆ who cares for the place

◆ what the pilgrim will find

◆ any hints to help the pilgrims make the most of their pilgrimage experience.

War graves in France.

First-hand information

Work in pairs

◆ Decide who you will interview.

Either: someone who has been on pilgrimage to Lourdes. This may be a sick person, a helper, a priest, a pilgrimage organiser, a doctor, a nurse, or someone who has been for the first time.

Or: someone who has been on pilgrimage to a holy place in the United Kingdom or Ireland (for example, Walsingham, Iona, Knock).

◆ Make a list of questions for your interview.

◆ Set a time for the interview.

◆ Reflect on and present your findings as a Fact File or Question and Answer Report.

Pilgrims at Lourdes.

Reflect

Though with great difficulty I am come hither, Yet now I do not repent me of all the trouble I have been at to arrive where I am.
(From *The Pilgrim's Progress*, John Bunyan)

Evaluate

From your work on pilgrims, what have you learned about people and their expectations?

On the way

In the early days of the Church, the people who had walked and talked with Jesus had a very special place. They were witnesses. They could tell people what he had said and done. They were disciples. They had shared Jesus' life and he had entrusted to them the work of telling the Good News to the whole world. After Pentecost, they set out on this mission and travelled through the known world. From the beginning they were clear that following Jesus was the Christian way. Every disciple was called to 'walk with' him.

Gradually, the Church came to understand that there are many ways of 'walking with Jesus'. The written gospels enabled people to walk with Jesus by listening to his words and teaching. In the celebration of sacraments people met the risen Jesus. The feasts and seasons of the Church's year became a pilgrimage with Jesus. People came to see that the whole of life is a pilgrimage with Jesus to God his Father.

Think back

Draw a timeline to show the sacraments as gifts for the Christian journey. How does each deepen the relationship of the disciple with Jesus?

Pilgrims all

As time went on, Christians began to journey to the 'Holy Land', to the places made holy by the life, death and resurrection of Jesus. It was as if seeing the hills he saw and walking the roads he walked helped them to feel close to him and understand him better. The physical journey could also be a spiritual journey.

A pilgrimage is a break from routine. The physical separation from all that is familiar can help people to focus on something special and important. In the Old and New Testament there are examples of people journeying into the desert in order to focus on God.

Early in the life of the Church, believers journeyed into the desert because they wanted to give their whole attention to journeying with Jesus. These desert fathers chose to live with only the bare necessities. They prayed long hours and fasted often. This did not stop them being very practical, and many people went out into the desert to ask for their advice.

This description of life as a pilgrim way comes from St Basil the Great, Bishop of Caesarea in the fourth century.

You are a traveller in this life. Everything goes past you and is left behind. You notice a flower on the way, or some grass, or a stream, or something worth looking at. You enjoy it a moment, then pass on. Maybe you come on stones, or rocks, or crags, or cliffs, or fences, or perhaps you meet wild beasts, or reptiles, or thorn bushes, or some other obstacles. You suffer briefly, then escape. That is what life is like. Pleasures do not last, but pain is not permanent, either. The 'way' does not belong to you, nor is the present under your control. But as step succeeds step, enjoy each moment as it comes and then continue on your 'way'.

(Commentary on Psalm 1)

In the twentieth century, another Basil, the Cardinal Archbishop of Westminster who died in 1999, also wrote about the pilgrimage of life as the search for meaning and for God.

There is something deep in each one of us which drives us on to search. What it is that we seek we do not always know. It is in part to understand, to know the reason for this pain, that hurt, the loss of one we love, the sickness which we witness, the loneliness which gnaws at the heart, the loss of hope, the despair of doubt. It is fear of the dark.

But there is another part, another urge, one which seeks and craves, craves that all manner of things should be well. It is the search for joy, for peace of mind, for happiness of heart. It is the love of light.

(*To be a Pilgrim*, Basil Hume OSB)

Work in groups

Discuss the two descriptions.
1 What do they have in common?
2 How does the imagery of each help readers to appreciate life as a pilgrim journey?
3 Using some of these ideas, create your own imagery to illustrate the pilgrim way of Christian life for
   (a) someone your own age or
   (b) a senior citizen.
   What symbols will you use to identify events in everyday life? For example, cliffs might symbolise hard choices; a stony path: feeling discouraged, or dark times; flowers: joyful meetings or times of light.
4 Record your ideas in words, images, art work, using ICT skills, as a poster or in other creative ways.

1A To be a pilgrim

The commandments

> Your word is a light for my steps, a guide for my path.
>
> *(Psalm 119)*

In the Old Testament there are several codes of law. The most famous is known as the Decalogue, God's ten words or commandments. *Deca* means 'ten' and *logos* means 'word'. There are two versions, one in Exodus (20:1–17) and the other in Deuteronomy (5:1–22).

For the Israelites God's law was a gift, part of the covenant by which the Israelites became the chosen People of God. The commandments were light for the People on their journey. To study the law was a privilege and joy for Jewish believers. Read Exodus 20:1–17.

The Sumerians and other Middle East people wrote their laws on tablets like this.

The Church's teaching version of the commandments:

1. I am the Lord your God: you shall not have strange gods before me.
2. You shall not take the name of the Lord your God in vain.
3. Remember to keep holy the Lord's day.
4. Honour your father and your mother.
5. You shall not kill.
6. You shall not commit adultery.
7. You shall not steal.
8. You shall not bear false witness against your neighbour.
9. You shall not covet your neighbour's wife.
10. You shall not covet your neighbour's goods.

Think and talk

1. Which commandments guide people in their relationship with God?
2. Which commandments guide people in their relationship with one another?
3. In pairs, choose one commandment. How would living out this commandment improve life for the Israelites? How might it help people today?
4. Look at the text from Exodus and the Church's teaching version. What is similar? What is different? Why do you think there are differences?

The commandments were the guide for Jesus as he grew up in Nazareth. They were his Jewish heritage. When he began his public ministry people wanted to know what he had to say about the law and commandments.

Read Mark 12:28–34.

≡ Classwork ≡

A. *Read Jesus' two commandments again. For each commandment, list five ways it would bring happiness and order for Christian disciples in their daily lives.*

B. *How does Luke show Jesus' respect for the commandments? How would Jesus' answer help people to understand the commandments better?*

C. *How do Jesus' two commandments contain all the ten? Use your design skills to present your answer.*

When Jesus sums up the commandments, he is challenging people to see that they are more than rules and regulations. They are not a burden, baggage to be dragged along on the journey. They challenge people to discover quality in life, to find joy on the pilgrimage, to have confidence in God who walks with his people, and to hope for the end of the journey.

Augustine of Hippo was an African bishop of the fifth century. His search for God was not easy, and he himself described the wrong choices he made. So he is speaking from experience when he says:

> There is not a person in this world who is not a voyager, even if not all are anxious to return to the homeland. In the course of this voyage the waves and the storms make us seasick, but at least we are in the ship.

Extension!

Commandments:

Copymaster [1]

Augustine found that he did not journey alone. Although each person's relationship with God is personal, the gospel message is that the Church is one Body. At times we all feel the need to 'go it alone'. At other times we need to know there is someone ready to walk with us. Each person's life journey brings times when we need physical, moral and spiritual support.

Augustine also wrote:

You have made us for yourself :. ☺ Lord and our hearts are restless until they rest in you.

══ **Homework** 🏛 ══

1. *Research St Augustine. Find out about some of the difficult choices that he had to make. Who and what helped him to find the right path?*

2. *What advice might he give to someone struggling to follow Jesus today? Use as your sources a dictionary of saints, and some of his writings in a modern version.*

3. *Write a letter to a pilgrim who is struggling on their journey. Choose from St Augustine's story or writings some things you think will encourage her or him.*

In light and darkness

Spiritual support can include having someone to talk to about the inner challenges and changes that come our way. Some people have a trusted friend, some a counsellor, some a spiritual companion or guide. Some lay people and priests train as spiritual companions. Many people choose to make a retreat. They will spend a few days, a week or even a month away from their job and home at a retreat centre. As well as extra time for prayer, they may spend some time talking things over with a spiritual guide. It can be a help to talk about prayer and God in a personal way.

Seeking God.

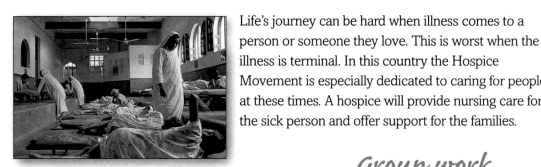

Mother Teresa's Home for the Dying in India.

Life's journey can be hard when illness comes to a person or someone they love. This is worst when the illness is terminal. In this country the Hospice Movement is especially dedicated to caring for people at these times. A hospice will provide nursing care for the sick person and offer support for the families.

In India Mother Teresa made the care of the dying a particular part of the work of her Order, the Missionaries of Charity. She and the sisters would go through the crowded streets and slums of Calcutta and collect the dying people they found there. They brought them to *Nirmal Hriday* – the House of the Pure Heart. It didn't matter what religion or *caste* they were. It didn't matter whether they had days or only hours to live. She wanted them to die with dignity and surrounded by love. She said, "We cannot let a child of God die like an animal in the gutter." In order to see Jesus in each person, she believed it was vital to spend time with him. Prayer was the heart of her work and she made it a rule for her sisters to spend an hour each day in silent adoration before the Blessed Sacrament.

Extension!

Plan and lead a year assembly on 'The Christian life journey'.

caste: Hindus believe each person is born into a different caste or group.

Group work

1 As a class, decide who will research Retreat Houses, the Hospice Movement, Mother Teresa's life and the sisters and co-workers of Mother Teresa.
2 Focus on your local area as much as possible. Your research should include:
   ◆ factual details of when and how the work began
   ◆ who does the work and how it is funded
   ◆ views and opinions of workers and volunteers
   ◆ views and opinions of those who come to the retreat house or hospice.

Why do people choose this work?
What part does Christian faith play in their choice?
Why is prayer important?
Decide how you will present your findings for the class to share.

Response

The Temple in Jerusalem was a place of pilgrimage for the Jewish people. As a child and an adult Jesus made this journey. Find Psalm 122, a pilgrimage psalm. What makes the pilgrims glad?

Reflect

Trust the past to the mercy of God, the present to his love, the future to his providence.
(St Augustine)

Glossary

Enter these words in your personal glossary with a brief explanation for each:

pilgrim
pilgrimage
commandments
guide
life journey
desert fathers

Assessment ?

1. *Why is pilgrimage a good image for the Christian life?*
2. *Name a place of Christian pilgrimage. Why would people choose to go there?*
3. *What are the first three commandments about?*
4. *What are some challenges of the seven commandments about love of neighbour?*
5. *What answer did Jesus give to the question about the greatest commandment?*

Living faith

O God, you search me and you know me.
All my thoughts lie open to your gaze.
When I walk or lie down, you are before me:
ever the maker and keeper of my days.

You know my resting and my rising.
You discern my purpose from afar.
And with love everlasting you besiege me:
in ev'ry moment of life or death, you are.

Before a word is on my tongue, Lord,
you have known its meaning through and through.
You are with me, beyond my understanding:
God of my present, my past and future, too.

Although your Spirit is upon me,
still I search for shelter from your light.
There is nowhere on earth I can escape you:
even the darkness is radiant in your sight.

For you created me and shaped me,
gave me life within my mother's womb.
For the wonder of who I am, I praise you:
safe in your hands, all creation is made new.

From Psalm 139, Bernadette Farrell

What hope for life's journey might a Christian find in this song version of Psalm 139? Perhaps you could find the music.

Or: Find another song of pilgrimage and search. Share your choice with the class.

Dilemma

Some parts of a journey can only be made alone.

Go further

A pilgrimage, or any journey, separates you from familiar things. Evaluate how this might be an advantage or a disadvantage.

1B Time challenges

Time travels

Think of a situation when you wanted time to pass quickly so things would change.

Think of a situation when you wanted time to stand still so things would not change.

Why did you feel like this?

What different emotions did you feel?

What happened to change your feelings?

How was the passing of time important in each situation?

What or who helped you to cope with the changes?

Time is:

too short for those who wait,
too long for those who fear,
too long for those who grieve,
too short for those who rejoice;
but for those who love,
time is eternity.

(Henry van Dyke)

Discuss how these feelings about time were part of the emotions you identified in your own situations.

For each scenario

Discuss what changes might time bring.

Use the following questions to help you.

◆ What kind of changes might there be?

◆ How will they affect the person involved?

◆ Who else will be involved?

◆ What developments can you foresee?

◆ Can you predict an outcome?

Change

Scenario one
Joe has had to go into foster care. His mother is in hospital after a car accident.

Scenario two
A multi-national company plans to open a drive-in food outlet. Mrs Britton is worried that the extra traffic will be dangerous for local children.

Scenario three
Mr Gardiner is going for an interview for a job that will mean moving house. His daughter Roz is angry because she may have to change school.

Reflect

To live is to change and to be perfect is to have changed often.

(John Henry Newman)

Reflect

Work in groups

Brainstorm themes that are common to these pictures.

Use the following questions to help you.

What do you see?

What has gone before?

What is in the future?

What was the person who took the photograph trying to capture?

For whom will the photograph have meaning?

Share your findings with the class.

Write about moments in your life when you have realised that you have changed. For example, you find an old exercise book or piece of artwork; you meet a relative who still treats you as if you were younger; you find clothes that you used to think were fashionable, a CD that now embarrasses you or videos you used to enjoy.

What other changes have you experienced – at home, academically, socially, physically, spiritually?

Draw up a list of **changes in your life**: the event, object, place or person which made you **realise** the change, how you **feel** about it (amused, embarrassed, uncomfortable, relieved) and anything you may have **learned** from the experience.

NB This work is private and confidential. For your eyes only.

Homework 🏛

History is now

Interview someone who has a memory of the Catholic Church: your parents, grandparents, a neighbour, a teacher, someone who knows the Church well.

What has been the biggest change in the Church since their young days?

What did they like about the change?

What did they find difficult about the change?

What or who helped them to cope?

Write a report of your interview. Include what you learned about the Church; and what you learned about how people cope with change. Were you surprised by any responses? Explain.

1

Change and challenge

In the history of the Church in England and Wales, time has brought change and development. In Year 8 you built up a picture of the history of the Church in England and Wales from Roman times to the beginning of the sixteenth century. Now you will investigate some of the changes and challenges that the Church faced over the next 500 years. The overview of key people and events will give you ideas for your own projects.

Think back

Brainstorm what you know about:
Bede
Augustine of Canterbury
Thomas a Becket
the Synod of Whitby

History in your pocket

If you look at a twenty pence piece you will see around the monarch's head the letters: DG REG FD – *Deo Gratia Regina, Fidei Defensor*, 'By the grace of God Queen, Defender of the Faith'. The Pope gave this title to Henry VIII in 1521. It was to acknowledge the King's defence of the sacraments against the attacks of a German monk named Martin Luther. Henry never gave up the title, yet within 15 years Parliament declared him to be Supreme Head of the Church in England and the Pope excommunicated him.

A modern and a Tudor coin.

Tudor Britain

Church and civil courts were struggling for control. In Britain and Europe, reformers, who came to be called, 'Protestants', challenged the Church's authority and teaching about sacraments. They took their stand on the authority of the Bible.

1533   Parliament recognised the king's power in law and the courts as sovereign.
Archbishop Cranmer declared Henry VIII's marriage to Catherine null and void. Henry married Anne Boleyn.

1534   Parliament named **Henry VIII** Supreme Head of the Church in England. The Act of Succession meant all subjects had to acknowledge Henry's divorce and marriage.
John Fisher and **Thomas More** were executed.

1535   The first **Tyburn martyrs** were hung, drawn and quartered.

1536   Dissolution of monasteries began.

1538   Henry ordered an English translation of the Bible to be put in every church.
Edward VI was committed to the Protestant cause.

The Tudor Rose.

1549   Publication of the **Book of Common Prayer** and 39 articles of faith.
Those loyal to the pre-Reformation faith were called Papists, loyal to the Pope.
Mary Tudor, daughter of Queen Catherine, was a committed Catholic.
Elizabeth I was committed to the independence of the Church in England.

1559   Protestant religion established by law. Every church had to display the royal arms and Elizabeth's birthday became a holy day. Those who did not attend a Protestant church on Sunday were fined.

The underground Catholic Church

Early martyrs.

Mass was forbidden. Priests were hunted down, tortured and executed. Anyone who attended Mass or helped and sheltered priests could be imprisoned, burnt at the stake or hanged, and their land and property would be confiscated. Many were prepared to take these risks. Young men went abroad to be trained as priests at Douai, Rome or Valladolid in Spain. They came back with new ideas. When they returned to England and Wales they found men and women faithful to their Catholic faith and ready to risk their lives for the sake of attending Mass. Forty of these martyrs of England and Wales were canonised by Pope Paul VI in 1970. *Copymasters* 4 5 6

Seventeenth and eighteenth centuries

James I of England (James VI of Scotland) was a Scottish Protestant.

1605 **The Gunpowder Plot** failed; fresh persecution of Catholics.

1611 **The King James Bible**, the authorised version for the Church of England, was published.

Groups of 'Dissenters' formed, those who did not agree with some of the ways of the Church of England.

The **Puritans** wanted simplicity in worship and banned all statues, candles and rituals. Oliver Cromwell was committed to the Puritan ideals.

John and Charles Wesley founded the **Methodists**. They led a revival within the Church of England. When they were no longer welcome, their movement became a separate Church.

George Fox and his followers formed the **Society of Friends** (Quakers).

The **Baptists'** understanding of faith meant that baptism could only be celebrated by persons who could profess their faith.

The **URC Church** brought together the heirs of the Dissenters.

Charles I was executed during the English Civil War.

Charles II was a Catholic in secret.

James II was openly Catholic.

1688 Parliament invited James' daughter **Mary** and her Protestant husband, **William of Hanover**, to become King and Queen of England.

1701 **The Act of Settlement**. The King or Queen of England and anyone in the line of succession could not be a Catholic and was not allowed to marry a Catholic.

Nineteenth and twentieth centuries

1829 Parliament passed the **Act of Catholic Emancipation**.

The Oxford Movement: Anglicans who wanted to be guided by Tradition as well as the Bible.

John Henry Newman and **Henry Manning** were received into full communion with the Roman Catholic Church and later both were named Cardinals.

1850 **The Restoration of the Catholic Hierarchy of England and Wales.**

Cardinal Nicholas Wiseman was the first Archbishop of Westminster.

Henry Manning, second Archbishop of Westminster.

1914 Outbreak of the First World War, ending in 1918.

1939 Outbreak of the Second World War, ending in 1945.
Barriers broke down as Protestants and Catholics fought and died together.

1B Time challenges

Change in the Church

While the Protestant Reformation was spreading, the Catholic Reformation of the sixteenth century brought reform and renewal to the Church. Some key events and people you might research are:

St Angela Merici
1474–1540

An Italian, daughter of a farmer, she became the leader of a group of women dedicated to a Christian life, works of charity and especially the education of young girls. She was the founder of the Ursulines.

The Council of Trent, 1545-1563

This was the longest Council in Church history. In 25 sessions it covered matters of concern raised by the Protestant challenge and social changes. These included the place of Scripture and Tradition, the seven sacraments and their place in Christian life, and the need for priestly education. One of the results of the Council was a Catechism for priests.

St Ignatius Loyola
1491–1556

This Spanish nobleman founded the Society of Jesus, the Jesuits. Several of the 40 martyrs were Jesuits trained in Rome for the English mission.

St Teresa of Avila
1515–1582

This Spanish Carmelite nun led the reform of her order.

Over to you: class projects

Choose from the timeline for individual projects. For example, Henry VIII and the Break with Rome, the Underground Catholic Church, profiles of one or two of the 40 Martyrs, key events or key figures of the Catholic Reformation or of more recent times. Plan your project to include:

– key people, key dates, key events, key statements by
  the people or about them
– what changes came about as a result of these people and events
– who was affected by the changes and how
– how people coped with the changes
– your evaluation of what the changes meant for the Church in England
  and Wales.

Display and share your work.

Change and development are essential for the life of the Church. Some key events for the Church in modern times:

1848 **Pope Pius IX** had to escape from Rome to France and could only return under the protection of the French army.

1870 **The First Vatican Council**, the first ecumenical council for 300 years. It was interrupted by war and ended before it completed its business. It discussed the role and authority of the Church and infallibility.

Before it could finish its discussion, war broke out and the Council was suspended indefinitely.

1962–1965 **The Second Vatican Council** was called by Pope John XXIII. After his death the Council's work continued under the guidance of Pope Paul VI.

The Council's vision and teaching were published in 16 documents. The renewal of the Church it called for continued in the renewal of the Liturgy, the publication of the Code of Canon Law and, in 1992, the publication of the Catechism of the Catholic Church, the first Catechism for the whole Church since the Council of Trent.

In his Letter introducing the Catechism Pope John Paul II wrote that it would 'make a very important contribution to the work of renewing the whole life of the Church as desired and begun by the Second Vatican Council'.

Infallibility means that the Church is protected from error when teaching in matters of faith or morals. The First Vatican Council applied this infallibility to the Pope when he defines a question of faith or morals. For example, in 1950 Pope Pius XII defined the Assumption of Mary, Mother of Christ.

A Council is an occasion when the Pope teaches infallibly. He does this when he endorses the Council's documents.

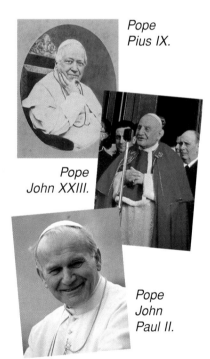

Pope Pius IX.

Pope John XXIII.

Pope John Paul II.

Classwork

A. *Write a letter to the person you interviewed about the changes in the Church (p.15). Choose two or three key people or events that you think changed the history of the Church and explain what you have learned about them and why they were important.*

B. *Prepare two handouts or overheads that could be used to introduce a lesson for a Year 8 class about changes in the Church.*

C. *Using evidence from the class project work write a two-column magazine article on 'Changes in the Church: Blessings or Blunders?'*

Extension

Discuss: what are some of the challenges that face Christians in the troublespots of the world today?

1B Time challenges

Response

Reflect

No pain, no gain.
What gain has pain brought
to the Church?

Reflect

Assessment ?

1. *Give three reasons why change is essential for the development of a community.*

2. *Nominate three people for an award to recognise their part in the history of the Church in England and Wales. Write one sentence about each to support your choice.*

3. *Who were the 40 Martyrs? Name two.*

4. *When were the Catholic dioceses of England and Wales restored?*

5. *Which Pope called the Second Vatican Council?*

Glossary

Enter these words in your personal glossary with a brief explanation for each:

**Reformation
persecution
religious movement
the King James Bible
infallibility
Ecumenical Council
Vatican II
Catechism**

Dilemma

Thomas More greeted the news of his execution with these words:

"I die the King's good servant, but God's first."

Living faith

"In you we live and move and have our being."

What do these words say about God's relationship with time?

World Youth Day, Rome, 2000.

Go further

What next? Identify some present-day changes that you think challenge the Church as it faces the future.

Leadership challenges

The Leader
I wanna be the leader
I wanna be the leader
Can I be the leader?
Can I? I can?
Promise? Promise?
Yippee, I'm the leader
I'm the leader
OK what shall we do?
Roger McGough, Poems on the Underground

Discuss

So ... what does a leader do?
What kind of leader will this person be?

Leaders

Imagine that you have been asked to
nominate people for the following positions:
◆ Manager of a national football team
◆ Prime Minister of Great Britain
◆ Secretary General of the United Nations.

Who would you nominate?
Give reasons why people should
vote for your choices.

Discuss

How do we know when a leader is doing a good job?
What happens when leaders let people down? Give examples.
How does the leadership style affect how people hear
the message?
How does the leadership style affect how people respond?
For example, his or her way of speaking, tone of
voice, treating everyone fairly.

Imagine your school is to appoint a new headteacher.
Work with a partner to come up with a list
of four questions that you would want to ask.
What would you be looking for in the
answers to these questions?

Extension

Design a job advert for a
headteacher for your school.

**In this section of
our work we will
be learning:**

◆ how leaders influence people
◆ what the Jews expected the
  Messiah to be
◆ how Jesus challenges these
  expectations.

Create a Wordstore

A good leader will:
  support
  encourage
  have vision.

Add your own ideas to this list.

Think back

Which Jewish religious groups
at the time of Jesus would
have lined up behind
these banners?

SAFEGUARD JEWISH TRADITION   SMASH THE ROMANS

The Messiah

The Jews were waiting for a leader. They were waiting for God to send them the longed-for Messiah. The Hebrew word *Messiah* and the Greek word *Christ* both mean 'the Anointed One'. Pouring holy oil over the head of a prophet, high priest or king was anointing. This showed that they were specially chosen by God for their work.

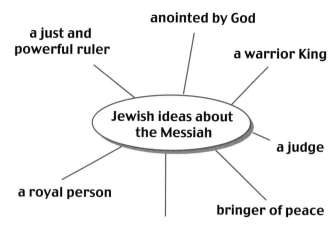

Eventually the title Messiah was used to identify a specially anointed person, a future King, who would bring about God's rule and make Israel a great nation again. The Messiah would free the people from oppression and bring peace on earth.

Expectations of the Messiah

There are many passages in the Hebrew Scriptures, the Christian Old Testament, where promises are made about a leader that God would send who would establish a great kingdom. For example, 2 Samuel 7:12–15, tells of the promise made to David that one of his sons would have a special mission and be special to God: "I will be his father and he will be my son."

Christ, from Michaelangelo's 'Last Judgement', Sistine Chapel, Rome.

The Book of Daniel

This book could be described as underground resistance literature. It was written to give courage and hope to those who were determined to be faithful at all costs. It uses symbolic language and contains visions describing the 'Son of Man':

> I gazed into the visions of the night.
> And I saw coming on the clouds of heaven,
> one like a son of man.
> He came to the one of great age and was led into his presence.
> On him was conferred sovereignty, glory and kingship,
> and all peoples, nations and languages became his servants.
> His sovereignty is an eternal sovereignty that shall never pass away, nor will his empire be destroyed.
>
> Daniel 7

Jesus used the title 'Son of Man' most frequently when speaking about himself. He did not claim the title 'Messiah' publicly. He was aware of the Jewish expectations and some common misunderstandings.

Jesus the Messiah

The Church applies Old Testament descriptions of the Messiah to Jesus, the One who fulfils the promise of the Saviour. The prophecies offered hope and encouraged God's people. The Messiah would come and save them. He would bring peace. He was also a mysterious figure. In the Book of Isaiah there are four poems called the 'servant songs'. The longest, the 'Song of the Suffering Servant', speaks of the servant of God who endured suffering and death for the sake of others. Read Isaiah 52:13–53:12.

Isaiah also spoke about the Messiah as a healer: 'The blind will be able to see, and the deaf will hear. The lame will leap and dance, and those who cannot speak will shout for joy.' (Isaiah 35:6)

The Holy Night, Maratta, after 1652.

The Entry into Jerusalem, Fra Angelico, 1450.

≡ Homework 🏛 ≡

Either: choose one of the scripture passages you have read. Why do you think the Church applies this passage to Jesus?

Or: write a character sketch of the Messiah using these scripture passages as your source material.

In Year 8 you studied Mark's description of the baptism of Jesus (Mark 1:9–13).

Mark is telling believers that Jesus was sent by God his Father and empowered by the Holy Spirit. For Mark, Jesus' baptism is a sign that the Kingdom of God has come (Mark 1:15).

Matthew, in his gospel, probably written for a Jewish Christian community, proclaims Jesus as the Messiah who fulfils the Old Testament prophecies.

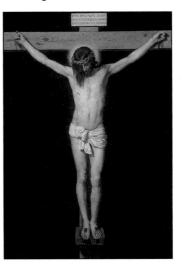

Christ on the Cross, Diego Velazquez, 1599–1660.

Work in groups

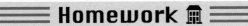

1 Match the verses from Matthew's gospel and the Old Testament prophecies. Decide what each promise is and how it is fulfilled in Jesus.

Matthew's Gospel	Old Testament Passages
12:18–21	Isaiah 42:1–4
21:4–5	Isaiah 62:11 and Zechariah 9:9
1:23	Isaiah 7:14
4:15–16	Isaiah 8:23–9:1
8:17	Isaiah 53:4
2:6	Micah 5:1

2 Improvise a dialogue between Matthew and a group of Jewish believers who are hearing about Jesus for the first time.

1C Leadership challenges

Jesus made no claim to Messiahship in the early part of his *ministry*. He even told his disciples and some of those he had cured not to tell anyone that he was the Christ. He realised that if he was proclaimed Messiah, people would want to make him fit their ideas of a warrior figure. He wanted people to listen to what he had to say, see what he did, and so understand what kind of Messiah he was to be. He taught his disciples that he had come to do the work of his Father.

ministry: Jesus' mission, his work among the people

Misunderstandings

Among the disciples there were misunderstandings about the kind of Messiah Jesus was.

- James and John asked for the best seats in the Kingdom of Heaven. (Mark 10:35–45. NB, Matthew says it was the mother of James and John who did the asking.)
- Some of the disciples argued about which of them was the greatest (Mark 9:33–37).
- Peter could not understand how Jesus could possibly suffer and die for others (Matthew 16:21–26).
- Even after the resurrection, some disciples thought the kingdom was a political one (Acts 1:6).

Look up and read the Scripture passages.

1. How did Jesus go about helping the disciples to see what being a disciple and a leader really meant?

2. Select and write down a key sentence from each passage that sums up Jesus' message for the disciples about himself and the kind of Messiah he was.

Fact file:

- Jesus was the Messiah who was:
  sent by God
  the Son of God who prayed 'Abba', Father
  of King David's line
  a teacher and healer
  the Anointed One.
- He brings a message of peace and love.
- His message is for the world, not just Israel.
- His message is spiritual, not just worldly.

═══ Classwork ═══

A. *Choose one image of Jesus as Messiah that you feel has an important message today. Explain why.*

B. *Under two headings list key facts you have learned about:*
   Jesus the Messiah
   Jewish expectations of Messiah.
   What is the same? What is different? What two questions might the Jews want to ask Jesus?

C. *Design a promotional leaflet, 'Jesus the Messiah', for a retreat day for young people. Include one quotation from the Scripture you have explored that sums up your ideas about Jesus the Messiah.*

Response

Glossary

Enter these words in your personal glossary with a brief explanation for each:

Christ
Son of Man
of David's line

Dilemma

Without a vision the people perish.

What do you think this means? What part does a leader play in shaping and promoting a vision?

Reflect

> Hallowed be thy name – not mine.
> Thy kingdom come – not mine.
> *(Dag Hammarskjold, United Nations Secretary General 1953–61)*

Reflect

Assessment ?

1. *What does the word 'Messiah' mean?*
2. *Give two examples of Jewish expectations of the Messiah.*
3. *How was Jesus' understanding of the Messiah different?*
4. *What was Jesus' favourite title for himself?*
5. *Give one example of how Matthew's gospel shows Jesus as the one who fulfils the Old Testament prophecies.*

Living faith

I, the Lord of sea and sky,
I have heard my people cry.
All who dwell in dark and sin,
My hand will save.
I, who made the stars of night,
I will make their darkness bright.
Who will bear my light to them?
Whom shall I send?

Here I am, Lord.
Is it I, Lord?
I have heard you calling in the night.
I will go, Lord,
if you lead me,
I will hold your people in my heart.

I, the Lord of snow and rain,
I have borne my people's pain.
I have wept for love of them.
They turn away.
I will break their hearts of stone,
Give them hearts for love alone.
I will speak my word to them.
Whom shall I send?

I, the Lord of wind and flame,
I will tend the poor and lame.
I will set a feast for them.
My hand will save.
Finest bread I will provide till their
	hearts be satisfied.
I will give my life to them.
Whom shall I send?

'Here I Am, Lord', Dan Schutte, SJ

What does this hymn say about the mission of the Messiah?
What does it say about how Christians can share this mission?

1D Prayer challenges

Time talk: *Copymaster* 7

Discuss some contemporary attitudes to time.

Targeting time

A profile of Jo
Year 9 student: represents county in sport; plays guitar in a group; member of school drama group; about to start Duke of Edinburgh bronze award; has to travel an hour each way to get to school; family are enthusiastic cyclists; is expected to prepare evening meal one day a week.

A profile of Nicky
Year 9 student: is falling behind; spends hours watching TV or videos or messing about in the shopping centre with mates; helps at the animal hospital when allowed; has to help with family shopping; would like to revise for exams and is thinking about catch-up sessions being held after school; would prefer to leave school.

Reflect
More haste, less speed.

Reflect

Think back
1. What evidence can you offer to show that people of all cultures and religions take time out for prayer?
2. Name three forms of prayer common to Catholics.

Discuss
1. Evaluate the extent to which Jo and Nicky have time for themselves, for prayer, for friends and family.
2. What changes and priorities would you suggest to help each of them manage their time? Why?
3. Plan a weekly timetable for Jo and Nicky. You will need to include time for study, homework, revision for exams, family and friends, prayer and relaxation.

Through Jesus Christ our Lord

No Christian prays alone. Every Christian who prays is united with the prayer of Jesus and the whole family of the Church. The heart of all prayer is the loving relationship of Jesus with God his Father. Jesus invites his disciples to be one with him and pray 'Our Father'. The word he used for 'father' is a familiar, informal word, closer to our word 'Dad'.

This unity is most clear in the Church's *liturgy*. The formal prayers of the Church are addressed to God the Father and commonly end with the words 'Through Jesus Christ our Lord'. In the liturgy the Church is united with Jesus Christ. Remember the anointing with chrism at Baptism. Every Christian is called to share Christ's mission as:

◆ priest, in worship of God
◆ prophet, in proclaiming God's word
◆ king, in service of God's people.

liturgy: public service in the name of and on behalf of the people; public worship

The liturgical year is shaped by the life of Jesus. The readings, prayers and blessings of each season express the Church's faith in him and invite Christians to deepen their relationship with him.

Info file

The full ending of liturgical prayers is 'Through Jesus Christ our Lord, who lives and reigns with you in the unity of the Holy Spirit, one God for ever and ever'.

The Liturgy of the Word for Sundays follows a three-year cycle: Years A, B and C. The readings for weekday masses follow a two-year cycle: Years 1 and 2.

Classwork

Seasonal prayers and blessings:
Copymaster 8

A. *Work with a partner or in a group.*
Use coloured highlighters to identify one word or phrase that you think best expresses what each liturgical season celebrates. Look for: Advent, Christmas, Lent , Easter, Pentecost.

B. *Choose one liturgical season and research other examples of liturgical prayers, music, hymns, seasonal colours, symbols and images. What changes in mood are reflected and how? Use your findings to produce a prayer leaflet for this season. Illustrate it with appropriate images of the liturgical season and the natural season of the year when it occurs. Display the class work under the title:* Through the Year with Jesus Christ.

C. *Choose one of the following times: Time of Famine, Dedication (Blessing) of a Church, After the Harvest. Suggest prayers, readings and hymns for a Mass. Use at least one of the following sources for ideas: prayer books, missal, lectionary.*

Prayer comes from the heart

There is also a very personal dimension to prayer. Every relationship grows through communication, and prayer is relationship with God. Each person has to find his or her own way to pray and this can change during a lifetime. Some people find it easier to pray as part of a group. Some people prefer to be alone with God in silence. Some see service of others as a form of prayer.

Some common forms of prayer

A group at prayer.

Nuns at Tyburn.

Meditation

Christians meditate using words of Scripture, a prayer, a picture or the rosary. It helps to be in a quiet, comfortable atmosphere (not so comfortable that you fall asleep, nor so physically uncomfortable that you are distracted).

Often people will go away on retreat for a few days in order to have time for meditation. They may go to a poustinia. The name comes from a Russian word that means 'a place apart'.

Meditation can focus by the repetition of a single word, like 'Jesus', or a phrase such as 'You are my light and my help'. The disciples saw and heard Jesus pray like this. Read Mark 1:35.

At other times people will use their imagination to visualise a scene from the life of Jesus and put themselves into the picture. Silence can be a way into meditation and so can music.

Praise

Praise is prayer that focuses on the goodness and greatness of God.

◆ Read Isaiah 6:3 and Revelation 4:8. How does the Church use this prayer in the Mass?

Praise often takes the form of singing. The singing before and during sporting events is the fans' praise of their team!

Some of the most famous praise songs are the psalms. They are based on an antiphonal style of prayer. This means two choirs or sides say or sing the prayer, alternating line by line. In the psalms you will find that the lines often echo one another.

◆ Look up Psalms 134, 135 and 136. Thanksgiving is part of praise.

◆ Find your own examples of psalms of praise and thanksgiving. Choose one. What is the psalmist giving thanks for?

Extension

Gregorian chant is a distinctive form of Church singing. In some monasteries, monks and nuns sing the Prayer of the Church (Divine Office) at regular times each day. Find and listen to some examples of this.

Intercession

Intercession is prayer that focuses on others. The Prayers of Intercession at Mass are often called the bidding prayers. They concentrate on the needs of the community, local and global. There is a formula for these prayers. The invitation "Let us pray for ..." invites people to unite in prayer to God the Father for a need, a person or group of people. There is a silence for everyone to pray. Then all are invited to express their unity in prayer with the response: "Lord hear us." R. "Lord graciously hear us."
Or: "Lord, in your mercy." R. "Hear our prayer."

Prayer time

Is prayer for everyone?
In answer to the question "When do you pray?" a lot of people say, "When I'm driving". They often mean that is when they have time to themselves. In such a busy world, could there be any place for St Paul's advice: "Pray without ceasing"?

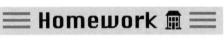

≡ Homework 🏛 ≡

Write a set of bidding prayers for a school celebration of Family Fast Day or some other local celebration.

1. Plan and carry out an audit among Year 9 students on attitudes to prayer, favourite times, places and words of prayer. The following questions may help you.
   What opportunities are there in school for formal prayer, personal prayer, different kinds of prayer?
   What do students want?
   What do students like about what is offered?
   What else would they like?
2. Display your findings.
3. Share your findings and prepare your conclusions and recommendations. Present these to your head of year or chaplain as a written or verbal report.
4. Draw up a class list of 'Tips for prayer' and/or 'Favourite prayers'. Add this to your display.

1D Prayer challenges

Icons

The Eastern Church has a tradition of using icons as a means for meditation and prayer. They have been called 'windows into heaven'. Icons are used with reverence and respect as holy things.

The making of an icon is prayer. The icon painter prepares for his or her work by meditation, prayer and fasting. Only natural materials are used, for example, vegetable dyes are used for the colours and egg yolk is used for fixing the colours. This expresses Christian faith that Jesus is God made man to share our life. Human life is holy: to live is holy. God's natural creation is holy.

Resurrection Icon: Christ is shown freeing Adam and Eve from the power of death and hell.

Class project

Research icons. Why do you think they are called 'windows into heaven'?

Aids to prayer

How can each of these be used as an aid to prayer?

Reflect

I see his blood upon the rose; and in the stars the glory of his eyes.

(Francis Thompson, poet, 1859–1907)

Reflect

Extension

"Prayer is a one-to-one with God."
Write an essay exploring this view, including your own opinion and giving reasons for your point of view.

Response

For many people prayer is time out, and their sense of proportion comes from God. What do you think?

Glossary

Enter these words in your personal glossary with a brief explanation for each:

meditation
praise
retreat
intercession
congregation
chant

Reflect

About 500 years ago, Leonardo da Vinci, the artist and scientist, said:

"Every now and then, go away, take a little relaxation, because when you come back to your work, your judgement will be surer. To remain constantly at work will cause you to lose your power of judgement. Go some distance away, because then the work appears smaller and more of it can be taken in at a glance, and a lack of harmony or proportion is more readily seen."

Reflect

Assessment ?

1. *Write three sentences about the Church's prayer.*
2. *What is a poustinia?*
3. *How are icons used for prayer?*
4. *Identify an aid to prayer and say how it might be used.*
5. *Give examples of how praise and intercession are used in Mass.*

Reflect

These are some ideas about prayer.

Which do you think would most encourage a beginner?

Which do you think would most encourage someone tempted to give up praying?

Pray as you can, not as you can't.

In prayer, everyone is a learner.

Prayer is conversation with God.

She who sings prays twice.

Prayer is action. Action is prayer.

Prayer is praise of God.

Prayer is silence.

A priest noticed an old man who regularly sat silently in church before the Blessed Sacrament for long periods of time. One day he asked him what he was doing. The old man replied, "I'm praying. I look at Him and He looks at me."

Reflect

Dilemma

Prayer is listening to God. How do I hear God?

Living faith

The life of prayer is the habit of being in the presence of God.

Go further

"'No' is also an answer." What advice would you offer someone who says she has given up praying because her prayers are never answered?

1D Prayer challenges

1E Hope challenges

Looking ahead

1. Make a list of your ambitions, the things you would like to achieve in the next 10–15 years.
   Think about some of the following and try to be realistic:

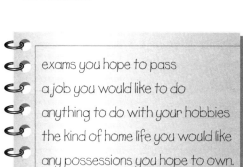

exams you hope to pass

a job you would like to do

anything to do with your hobbies

the kind of home life you would like

any possessions you hope to own.

2. What will you need to do to make these 'dreams' come true?
3. Now make a list of the hopes that your parents/carers and teachers have for you.
4. Compare the lists. Are they very similar or different?
5. Share your findings with others. Take note of what they have to say!

Read the story of **The Epics**.
Copymaster [9]

Answer the following questions:

1. Which of the following did The Epics need to achieve what they did? Patience, laziness, leaving everything to the last minute, hope, determination, wanting everything to happen now.
2. Find evidence in the interview to support your answers.
3. Why do you think relationships in the band and with families sometimes got 'a bit tense'?
4. How did Mrs Jones help The Epics?
5. Do you agree that the band's success was 'sweeter' because of all the effort it had taken? Give reasons for your answer.

Reflect

What is the difference between hope and expectation?
Hope is the power of being cheerful in circumstances which we know to be desperate.

(G K Chesterton)

Extension

1 Have you had any experience like the young people in The Epics? If you have, write down what happened. If you have not, write a short story about someone who wanted to achieve something and succeeded in the end, although it took a lot of effort.
2 Share your story with a partner or in a group.
3 Evaluate your stories. Will the reader appreciate how important it is for people to have aims, hopes and dreams?

Think back

Copy out and complete this crossword.

Across

1. During Advent the Church .... for the birth of Jesus.
3. The Hebrew title meaning 'the anointed one'.
5. Advent takes place four .... before Christmas.

Down

1. In the Old Testament these people promised that God would send his chosen one.
2. The month during which Advent is celebrated.
4. This John got people ready for the coming of Jesus.

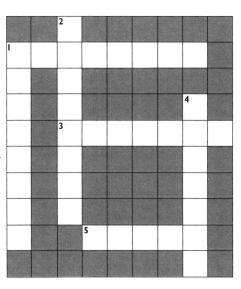

Reasons for living and hoping

Advent is the beginning of the Church's year. It leads directly to Christmas. The link between the two seasons is hope. To hope is to look forward, expecting that the good thing we hope for will happen. The Church believes that the coming of Jesus is the best of all events. He fulfils the deep hopes that are part of every human heart: for happiness, for peace, to be loved and to love, that are to be found fully only in God. The prayers and readings of Advent invite people to think about the amazing love that brought God into our world in the person of Jesus.

The 'O' Antiphons

The 'O' Antiphons have been part of the Prayer of the Church during Advent for centuries. They are said or sung at Evening Prayer for the seven days before Christmas. If you imagine the Gregorian chant of the antiphons in the darkness of a December evening, you may get some idea of the sense of the waiting, preparing and longing for the coming of Jesus that they express. They are prayers and words for meditation that call to mind the real meaning of Christmas. Study the 'O' Antiphons (p. 34) with the Glossary to help you.

Glossary

Antiphon:	a short song used as introduction to a psalm
Wisdom:	the loving kindness of God that draws all things together; here it is being used as a name for Jesus
Most High:	a name for God
Adonai:	a Hebrew word that means 'Lord'; Jews use this rather than speak God's sacred name
Root of Jesse:	'root' refers to Jesus' family tree; Jesse was the father of King David, Jesus was of the house and family of David (see Matthew 1:1–7 or Luke 2:1–5)
Dayspring:	poetic word for 'dawn' used as an Advent name for Jesus. When Luke writes about the prophecy of Zechariah, he describes the coming of Jesus as 'the bright dawn of salvation' (Luke 1:78–79)
Emmanuel:	A name for the Messiah meaning 'God-with-us'; see Isaiah 7:14. Matthew refers to this when he tells the story of Jesus' birth (Matthew 1:22–23).

O Wisdom, you came from the mouth of the Most High.
You fill the universe and hold all things in strength and gentleness.
O come, and teach us the way of truth.

O Adonai, and leader of Israel,
you appeared to Moses in a burning bush,
and you gave him the law on Sinai.
O come and save us with your mighty power.

O Root of Jesse, you stand as a signal for the nation:
Kings stand silent before you whom the peoples acclaim.
O come to deliver us and do not delay.

O Key of David and sceptre of Israel,
what you open, no one else can close again;
what you close, no one can open.
O come to lead the captives from prison,
from those who sit in darkness and in the shadow of death.

O Dayspring, you are the splendour of eternal life
and the sun of justice.
O come and enlighten those who sit in darkness
and in the shadow of death.

O King, whom all the peoples desire,
you are the cornerstone which makes us all one.
O come and save us whom you made from clay.

O Emmanuel, you are our King and judge,
the One whom the peoples await, and their Saviour.
O come and save us.

Collect your evidence:

1. What names are used for God? What idea of God do they create?
2. What is God asked to do? What hopes are expressed in these prayers?

Class project

Make a display of the 'O' Antiphons to put up in school during Advent. Think about the world today and include images, words, hopes and dreams for people throughout the world. *Or* make up your own 'O' Antiphons to display.

Extension

Christ will come again: Copymaster 10

≡ Classwork ≡

A. *Using the evidence you have collected, prepare a short Advent prayer service with one or two 'O' Antiphons as your theme.*

B. *Using the evidence you have collected, write a reflection for an Advent assembly titled 'Hope for the world'.*

C. *Choose one 'O' Antiphon that has a special message for the third millennium. Explain and illustrate your choice.*

Christmas time

The hope of the 'O' Antiphons is fulfilled when the Church celebrates Jesus' birth at Christmas. Christmas is celebrated with great joy because Jesus the Saviour has been born.

Homework 🏠

Examine some of the words of Christmas carols. Select examples of words or phrases that show what the Church celebrates. Are there any links with the messages of the 'O' Antiphons? Find a way to present your findings.

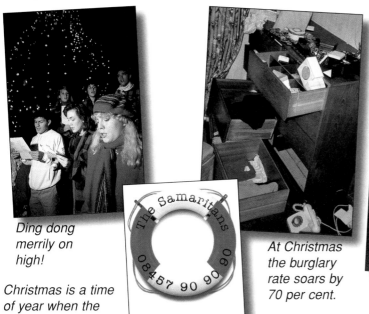

Ding dong merrily on high!

Christmas is a time of year when the number of phone calls rises.

At Christmas the burglary rate soars by 70 per cent.

Last year 2,000 volunteers gave their services for free.

Christmas is a world-wide feast, but for all the joy and celebration, it is clear that we do not live in a perfect world. There is still evil and suffering, pain and anger. How can this be if Jesus the Saviour was born at the first Christmas over 2,000 years ago?

Look at the photographs and discuss their messages.
1. What spoils people's Christmas celebrations?
2. What helps them to celebrate?
3. What evidence do you find here that people understand the real meaning of Christmas?
4. Look at the list in the box. How do these things make it easier or harder to celebrate Christmas as the feast of Christ's coming?

> spending money
> celebrating at parties
> the homeless
> lonely people
> sick people
> remembering the meaning of Christmas
> preparing to celebrate Christmas with the family
> war or disasters in parts of the world

Think and talk

"To see Christmas through its wrapping becomes more difficult with every year."

Do you think this is true or not? Give reasons.

Do you think it may have something to do with the freedom human beings have to choose whether the coming of Jesus is going to make any difference to them or not?

Reflect

Jesus is the guaranteed gift for rich and poor.

Response

Reflect

The hymn 'O Come, O Come, Emmanuel' is one of the most popular Advent hymns.

It is a popular version of the 'O' Antiphons.

Read, sing or listen to a recording of the hymn.

Have you ever hoped for anything this much?

Try writing an Advent hymn to express your hopes and what you are waiting for at Christmas.

Glossary

Enter these words in your personal glossary with a brief explanation for each:

hope
expectation
'O' Antiphons
Emmanuel

Assessment ?

1. *How does Advent celebrate past, present and future?*

2. *The prophets said the Messiah would be a descendant of which great Jewish king?*

3. *Give two of the names given to Jesus in the 'O' Antiphons.*

4. *Explain how the 'O' Antiphons are used during Advent.*

5. *Give an example of how the true message of Advent and Christmas challenges what goes on in the world at this time of year.*

Reflect

In Latin the first letters of the 'O' Antiphons read backwards make the word EROCRAS – "I will be with you tomorrow."

Dilemma

In 1652 the Puritan government of England abolished Christmas. Every kind of celebration and symbol was banned, from church services to mince pies. Christmas is not banned today, but when so many people ignore its real meaning, will it be long before it is abolished?

Living faith

The last words of the Bible:

Maranatha! – Come, Lord Jesus!

May the grace of the Lord Jesus be with everyone.

Go further

Evaluate how far the 'selling' of Christmas devalues the celebration of Advent.

Word made flesh

Suddenly one day

The Suzy Lamplugh trust was set up in December 1986 following the disappearance of estate agent Suzy Lamplugh whilst meeting an unknown client.

It is the national charity for personal safety. It aims to create a safer society and enable all people to live safer lives. "We want people of any age to enjoy their lives, but to do so safely," says Diana Lamplugh. Diana was one of the people who set up this trust as a direct result of her daughter's disappearance.

◆ Find out how the work has developed.
◆ Many helplines are set up as a direct result of a tragedy, in response to a need or to an experience that shocks a person into action. Research other helplines, why they were set up and what their aims are. For example, Childline; the Samaritans.

More often than you think, people survive life and death experiences. A traumatic experience will lead to a person either becoming stronger or diminished. The following accounts are true accounts of two people's life-changing experiences.

In 1989 Jerry Schemmel was a passenger on a plane flying from Denver to Chicago.

Jerry and his best friend had been on standby. They were the last of the 296 passengers to be given seats. Jerry agreed to swap seats with a boy so that he could sit with his father.

When the rear engine of the plane blew up, the pilots managed to bring the plane to land at a nearby airport. Jerry described what then happened as "raw chaos", as a fireball shot through the cabin. Many seats were ripped out and the plane was split in two, killing his friend and others in the row where he would have been sitting.

One hundred and twelve people died in the crash. Jerry now says that the experience changed his life and he feels a different person: "Forever changed, blessed and reborn," he says.

> ### In this section of our work we will be learning:
>
> ◆ about life-changing events
> ◆ about the transforming power of Jesus
> ◆ about the challenge of Jesus and his question "Who do you say I am?"

Diana Lamplugh.

Unit 2 At the heart of belief

37

2

Margaret Crotty was working in the East in 1996 for Save the Children. She was travelling from village to village, leading empowerment for women. She was on a crowded ferry when it ran into problems and started to sink.

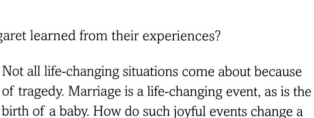

"The boat was going down," she says. "There was this disbelief. I was thinking 'This is what it is like to die'. It was dark. The boat was under water and I was inhaling water. I eventually managed to swim to the surface. There were people all around me." After surviving this terrible experience, Margaret says that she is now more focused than before. She is less willing to put up with dishonesty from others. She works in an inner city school. "Everything I've learned from that experience," she says, "I use in everyday life."

What do you think that Jerry and Margaret learned from their experiences?

Jacqueline du Pré.

Not all life-changing situations come about because of tragedy. Marriage is a life-changing event, as is the birth of a baby. How do such joyful events change a person's life?

A very famous cellist, Jacqueline du Pré, said, "The first time I heard a cello I said 'I want to play that sound'." She became what some describe as a genius on the cello before dying of multiple sclerosis in 1987, at the age of 42. It was listening to the radio at the age of five that set the course of her life.

Carpe diem is the Latin for 'Seize the day'. In the film *Dead Poets' Society*, the teacher constantly uses this phrase to urge his students to think carefully and choose what they really want to do.

◆ Discuss how easy it is or how difficult to recognise opportunities to 'seize the day'.
◆ Look back over your life and reflect on changes that have taken place.
◆ Use artwork or music to illustrate different parts of your life and the events that have made you the person that you are today.

Reflect

I shall be telling this with a sigh
Somewhere ages and ages hence:
Two roads diverged in a wood and I
– I took the one less travelled by,
And that has made all the difference.

from 'The Road Not Taken' by Robert Frost

Jesus makes a difference

John begins his gospel with a hymn of praise of Jesus and his place at the centre of human history. His disciples saw in him 'the glory of the only Son of the Father' (John 1:14). They also saw what it meant to be fully human, living in communion with God. These are three accounts from John's gospel that show how Jesus' words and actions transformed people's lives.

Work in groups. Read the passage and answer the question for each.

1. The woman at the well, John 4:1–42
   How did Jesus challenge her? How did she respond?
2. Lazarus, John 11:1–44
   How did this experience challenge Lazarus' sisters?
   What did it mean for Lazarus?
3. The man born blind, John 9: 1–41
   How did his neighbours and parents react
   to what had happened to him?

"Who do people say that I am?" (Matthew 16:13–16). Jesus puzzled people. He intrigued them. They wanted to see him. They asked questions about him. One day Jesus asked his disciples, "Who do people say that I am?" They replied: "Some say that you are John the Baptist, others say Elijah, and others Jeremiah or one of the prophets."

Then Jesus asked them a very direct question. "Who do you say that I am?"

Simon Peter spoke up and said: "You are the Messiah, the Son of the Living God."

Think back

What does the title 'Messiah' mean? What type of Messiah were the Jews waiting for?

What happened next?
Read Matthew 16:17–20. What did Jesus say about Simon Peter and what did he mean? Jesus was very happy about Peter's statement. Why? Why do you think that Jesus changed his name? Jesus then charged the apostles not to tell anyone that he was the Messiah. Why do you think he did this?

Extension

"Who do you say I am?" Write the responses Lazarus, the woman at the well and the man born blind might have made to this question.

Interpret the text

Present either a role-play or an interview showing how Jesus transformed the life of Lazarus, the woman at the well or the man born blind. Emphasise the difference that Jesus made to each one.

Christian tradition represents Peter with the 'keys of the kingdom'.

Homework 🏛

Find other examples from the gospels of how Jesus changed people's lives. Make notes. Present your findings in words – a poem or short essay; or images – graphic design or illustration.

2 Jesus, the Saviour for all time

Christians believe that Jesus is risen. He is alive and his transforming work continues in the Church by the power of the Holy Spirit. Jesus transforms and challenges people today just as he did 2,000 years ago. He still asks: "Who do you say I am?"

1. Research: ask people how they would answer Jesus' question. Include Christians of different ages and, if you can, people of other faiths.
2. Share your findings with the rest of the class and make a display of your answers in a central place.

Reflect

How would you have answered the question five years ago? How would you answer today? Why is it important for every Christian to answer this question for him or her self?

Reflect

The Church believes that Jesus makes a difference to the whole history of the human race: not just forward from when he was born, but back to the very beginning of time. Remember John's hymn of praise: 'In the beginning was the Word' and 'the Word was made flesh' (John 1:14).

The Son of God became 'one of us' and so he is 'at one' with every human being. Jesus does not just tell people about God's life and love. On the cross he gave his life in love and God his Father raised him to new life. This new life is for every single person who ever has lived or will live. Jesus takes the sins of humanity upon himself. He is numbered among criminals. He is unjustly condemned. He forgives the sins of those who inflict evil on others.

The Church, by the power of the Holy Spirit, makes known this good news. Jesus' life, death and resurrection overcome the power of evil and death. St Paul, in one of his letters, writes: "I am certain that nothing can separate us from the love of God made visible in Christ Jesus." (Romans 8:38)

Before printing, and before the majority of people had access to the Bible, this story of salvation was told in churches in stained glass windows and paintings. Today, the Misereor cloths are 'picture Bibles'. They use art styles from around the world. This is a cloth from Ethiopia.

Notes for the Misereor 'Hunger-Cloth': Copymaster [11]

Classwork

Study the cloth.

As a class, and with the help of your teacher, make brief notes on each of the frames so that you have a sense of the purpose of the whole cloth.

A. *Choose one frame that:*
- *tells of the **sinfulness** of human beings and the struggle between good and evil*
- *tells of the **hope** that God offers to those who listen*
- *tells of the **difference Jesus** makes to people's lives.*

Discuss in groups how the frames you have chosen tell a picture story of salvation.

B. *Design, in a series of five picture frames, a cloth that shows the issues and areas in the world today that need the power of God's saving love.*

C. *Choose one frame that would challenge a Christian to take Jesus seriously. Explain your choice.*

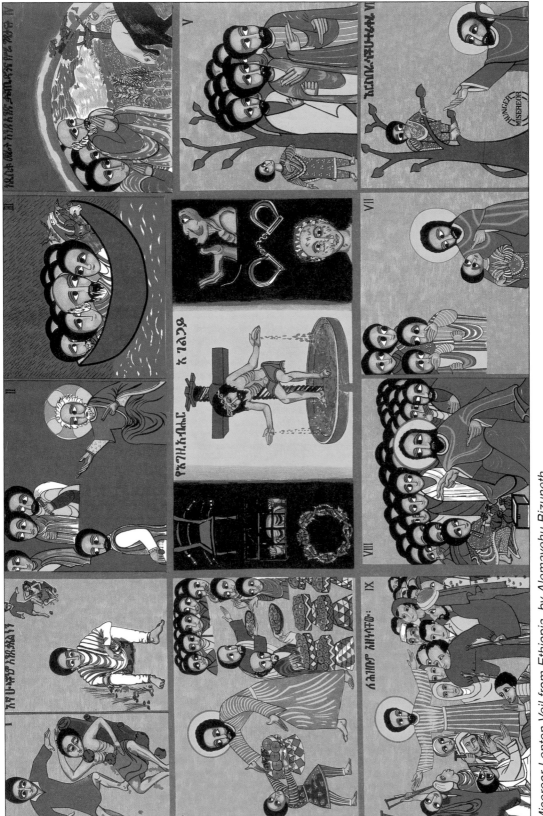

Misereor Lenten Veil from Ethiopia, by Alemayehu Bizuneth.

2A Word made flesh

Response

Reflect

What was Jesus like?

"I looked at the Gospel again, and quite suddenly a new portrait seemed to stare at me out of the pages. I had never previously thought of a laughing, joking Jesus, physically strong and active, fond of good company and a glass of wine, telling funny stories, using, as every good teacher does, paradox and exaggeration as among the most effective aids to instruction, applying nicknames to his friends, and holding his companions spellbound with his talk.

Imagine living your life in the companionship of this person who commands your love and adoration precisely because, having been through it all and sympathising with it all, he cheers you up and will not have you sad."

(Lord Hailsham, *The Door Wherein I Went*)

Assessment ❓

1. *Name one occasion in John's gospel when meeting Jesus changed someone's life.*
2. *What was Peter's response to Jesus' question, "Who do you say I am?"*
3. *What did this response mean for (a) Peter and (b) the Church?*
4. *Why are keys a symbol for St Peter?*
5. *What is the message of the Misereor hunger cloth?*

Dilemma

I like your Christ, but I do not like your Christians, because they are too unlike your Christ.

(Mahatma Gandhi, Hindu leader)

Go further

Make the case 'For' and 'Against' following Jesus Christ in the third millennium. Give your answer in the form of an essay, notes or in a visual image.

Glossary

Enter these words in your personal glossary with a brief explanation for each:

transform
keys of the kingdom
Misereor hunger cloth

Living faith

From heaven you came,
helpless babe,
entered our world, your
glory veiled;
not to be served but
to serve,
and give your life that
we might live.

This is our God, the
servant king.
He calls us now to
follow Him,
to bring our lives as
a daily offering
of worship to the
servant king.
'The Servant King',
Graham Kendrick

Love

Brainstorm situations when the word 'love' is used.
Which suggest love to be 'passing', 'temporary'?
Which suggest love to be 'long-lasting'?

Research the lyrics of your favourite songs that speak about love. Bring some examples to share in class. Do you think these images and expressions of love give us a clearer or more confused understanding of love? Explain your reasons.

> ## In this section of our work we will be learning:
> ◆ about different meanings and uses of the word 'love'
> ◆ that Jesus makes possible new ways of loving God and one's neighbour.

How is this love?

Look at the five actions listed.
Each shows love in a different way. How difficult is each?
Make a judgement in each case by writing down a number between one and five, where one equals 'not at all' and five equals 'a lot'. Then write a sentence to explain your choice.

What does love demand in each of these situations?

◆ Visiting or writing to a grandparent.
◆ Helping a younger brother/sister with homework.
◆ Taking a turn at doing the washing-up.
◆ Babysitting when you could go out.
◆ Not joining in making fun of someone.

The language of love

The Greek language has four different words for love. In *The Four Loves*, C S Lewis offers these definitions:
Storge: the love of things and situations, for example, "I love sport".
Eros: being "in love", for example, "I love my wife or husband and want to spend my life with her or him".
Philos: the love between family and friends.
Agape: unconditional love, putting others before yourself, whether you like them or not.

Look back over the work you have done so far. Think of the situations when the word 'love' is used, think of the examples of lyrics you have shared in class. In what ways do you think there is confusion in our society over which 'kind' of love suits which situation?

Evaluate

What have you learned to expand or change the ideas you had about 'love' at the beginning of this section?

This is love

Jesus was very clear about his use of the word 'love' and what he meant by it. His actions spoke louder than any words he spoke. The night before he died, he gave his disciples an action lesson in love.

Read John 13:1–15, the washing of the feet.

Look at this picture by Sieger Köder, a famous German religious painter.

The Washing of the Feet, © Sieger Köder, Fusswaschung, 1989.

Focus on Jesus: his position.
What does his position signify?
Can you see the face of Jesus?
Why do you think the painter shows Jesus' face reflected in the dirty water?

Focus on Peter: his face, his hands.
What do you think he is feeling, thinking?
With a partner, and using the painting, role-play the dialogue between Jesus and Peter.

Focus on the table: what do you see?
What is the artist prompting you to bring to mind?
What connections can you make between what Jesus is doing and what the objects on the table signify?

Use your previous work in *Icons* to recall at least two statements about love in the Old or New Testament.

Classwork

One of the most famous descriptions of love ever given is St Paul's words in 1 Corinthians 13:4–8. He describes all the qualities of love in a community where all people are different.

A. *Read the passage. Give it a title. Take each aspect/quality of love and give examples of how the following people might put that love into action:*
   - *a parent*
   - *a son or daughter.*

B. *Look again at the picture of the washing of the feet. What kind of love is this, and how is it possible in our world today? Think of one situation in our world where love of this kind could change things. Explain how, and what would happen.*

C. *Think back to all the work you have done on Jesus. Choose three aspects of love from 1 Corinthians 13 and give examples of how Jesus taught and lived them, and challenged his followers to do the same.*

Reflect

A new commandment I give to you: that you love one another as I have loved you.

John 13:34

Reflect

Love comes first

The command to love was part of the Jewish Law. It was the first commandment. Jesus challenges people to see love of neighbour as the other half of the commandment to love God. Jesus himself, through his life, suffering and death, showed exactly what he meant by love.

Once, a teacher of the Law asked Jesus which was the greatest commandment.

Jesus replied, "The most important one is this: 'Listen, Israel! The Lord our God is the only Lord. Love the Lord your God with all your heart, with all your soul, with all your mind and with all your strength.' The second most important commandment is this: 'Love your neighbour as you love yourself.' There is no other commandment more important than these two." (Mark 12:28–31)

Group work

Discuss what makes these the greatest commandments. What is the connection between the Two Commandments and the Ten Commandments? Share your conclusions.

The parable of the Good Samaritan

Work with a partner.

The Christian vocation is God's call to live the kind of love Jesus showed. He loved his Father and his friends to the point of being ready to lay down his life for them. Luke, in his gospel, puts the question about the two commandments in a different context. In his account the questioner asks a second question: "Who is my neighbour?" Jesus' answer is a parable which, like all his parables, has a sting in the tale.

The Good Samaritan, Joseph Heinemann, c 1900.

The Samaritans and the Jews had no dealings with one another. Strict Jews, like the Pharisees and Saducees, would travel extra miles rather than go through a Samaritan village. Keep this in mind as you read the parable: Luke 10:29–37.

1. How does Jesus, in this parable, show what the second part of the great commandment demands?
2. How does his parable challenge people to widen their understanding of who is a 'neighbour'? Using the lesson of the parable, define 'neighbour'.
3. What shows that the Samaritan loved his 'neighbour' as himself?
4. What did it mean for Jews to be told to love the Samaritan as a neighbour?

Reflect

Love changes everything.

Real love

Through the centuries, the men and women who are the Church, the Body of Christ in the world, have tried to respond to Jesus' challenge. They have done this as individuals, groups and organisations.

St Francis of Assisi prayed and lived the kind of love Jesus demands of his followers. This version of the Prayer of St Francis is an invitation to reflect on what lies behind the words and how they challenge people to live out both parts of the great commandment.

Lord, make me an instrument of your peace
– make me open to the work of your Spirit
– let me be glad to be used by you, as your instrument, for my family, my friends, all those I meet.

Where there is hatred, let me sow love
– help me to see the good in situations
– help me speak words of praise and encouragement rather than criticism and gossip.

Where there is injury, pardon
– help me to be the first to move towards reconciliation
– help me not to nurse my hurt, but remember how I have been forgiven.

Where there is doubt, faith;
Where there is despair, hope
– help me not to give up
– help me not to give in.

Where there is darkness, light;
Where there is sadness, joy
– help me to believe that your light is greater than any darkness
– help me to bring joy to those who need comfort and support
– help me to remember that joy is the mark of your disciples.

Group work

Identify situations today, locally, nationally, internationally, where living the prayer of St Francis can bring Christ's love. Use at least one of the following sources: national or international newspapers, CAFOD's *fairground* magazine, a Catholic newspaper.

☰ Homework 🏛 ☰

1. *Choose one part of the Prayer of St Francis. Create a collage of words and pictures to illustrate how Christians are living it out today. Here are some ideas that may help you:*

   ◆ Agape *(look back to the description on p. 43).*

   ◆ *Unconditional love doesn't ask whether another person is loveable.*

   ◆ *Unconditional love doesn't ask whether he or she can love back.*

   ◆ *Unconditional love has 'no strings attached'.*

   ◆ *Unconditional love gives with no limits except the limits of love.*

2. *Why do you think most people would like to have someone love them with an unconditional love?*

3. *Do you think most people would like to be able to love unconditionally? Why, or why not?*

4. *What do you think it means to say 'gives with no limits except the limits of love'? (Think of when 'no' might be the most loving thing to say – what is sometimes called 'tough love'.)*

2B Love

Response

Reflect

I am full of compassion and kindness; slow to anger and overflowing with faithful and enduring love.
(Exodus 34:6)

The mountains and the hills may crumble, but my love for you will never end.
(Isaiah 54:10)

I have loved you with an everlasting love,
so I continue my faithfulness to you.
(Jeremiah 31:3)

God showed his love for us by sending his only Son into the world so that we might have life through him.
(1 John 4:9)

Whoever loves knows God because God is love.
(1 John 4:7)

Reflect

Glossary

Enter these words in your personal glossary with a brief explanation for each:

the greatest commandment
storge
eros
philos
agape
unconditional love

Making a difference

How might a Christian respond to the following situations:
- a homeless person asks for money
- some students keep some of their school charity sponsored walk money
- the school shop has been left unlocked
- racist and sexist language is used in school.

Remember: tough love.

Dilemma

Love and do what you will.
(St Augustine)

Living faith

Love is his word, Love is his way, feasting with all, fasting alone.
Living and dying, rising again. Love, only love is his way.
Richer than gold is the love of my Lord, better than splendour and wealth.
Love is his name, love is his law. Hear his command, all who are his.
Love one another, I have loved you. Love, only love is his law.

'Love is his Word', Luke Connaughton

Assessment

1. *What are the two great commandments?*
2. *What is Jesus' message in the washing of the feet?*
3. *Define Christian love.*
4. *How does Jesus define a 'neighbour' in the parable of the Good Samaritan?*
5. *What does the Greek word* agape *mean?*

Go further

Look back to the definition of love you wrote at the beginning of this section. In the light of what you have learned, is there anything you want to add or change in your definition? Explain your reasons.

Sacrifice

The greatest love

In a small village near Sarajevo, mortar bombs hit an orphanage. Three aid workers were killed and several children were seriously wounded, including one 10-year-old girl. There was no medical help available until a doctor and nurse arrived from a neighbouring village, with nothing but their basic medical kits. The girl was the most seriously injured, and without quick action she would die from shock and loss of blood.

In a mixture of the local language, French and impromptu sign language, the doctor and nurse explained the situation to the children and asked if anyone would be willing to give blood to help. After several long moments, a small hand slowly went up, dropped back down and then went up again.

"Thank you," said the nurse. "What is your name?"

"Serge," came the reply.

Serge lay stiff and silent as the needle was inserted and the transfusion began. After a while he gave a sob, then another, and finally cried silently, his eyes tightly shut and his fist in his mouth to stifle the sobs. The medical team became concerned, but when they asked, "Is it hurting?" Serge just shook his head and went on crying.

Just then a Yugoslavian nurse arrived. She spoke to the distressed child in his own language and listened to his reply. As she continued to speak gently to him, he stopped crying and looked at her first in wonder and then in relief.

The nurse said to the medical team, "He thought you had asked him to give all his blood so the little girl could live."

"But why would be willing to do that?" asked the doctor.

The nurse repeated the question to the little boy, then translated his answer, "She's my friend."

In this section of our work we will be learning:

- ◆ about sacrifice as part and parcel of life
- ◆ about the Eucharist that is the sacrifice of Jesus.

People make sacrifices in different ways throughout their lives. Often sacrifice and love go together.

1. Collect evidence of this from the stories of people you know and the media.
2. Make a class display of your evidence.
3. Use it to defend the statement that sacrifice and love often go together.

Reflect

Love and sacrifice

People honour the soldiers who gave their lives for the sake of others. They also question the pain and waste of war. How much difference did the death of any one soldier make to the war? Can wartime enemies be forgiven for what they did?

The giving of Jesus on the cross reveals love and sacrifice that are unique. He is the Son of God offering himself to the Father for the forgiveness of the sins of the world. He gives his life for people who are enemies, who do not deserve it, who have tortured, killed, hated and refused to show love for others. In his death, goodness responds to evil with love and forgiveness. Everyone who asks "Can I be forgiven?" can find hope in the sacrifice of Jesus.

Do this in memory of me

The Mass, the Sacrament of the Eucharist, is the Church's living memory of the sacrifice of Jesus. It took time for the Church to understand this and realise that the Mass is the heart of its life. It took time for the sacramental celebration to take shape. In the next section of work you will:

◆ trace the story of this living memory and
◆ study how and why the Church celebrates this sacrifice.

Imagine three conversations with Simon, one-time fisherman of Galilee.

AD20

"Simon, tell us something about yourself and how you pray."
"I am a fisherman and a Galilean. I worship the Lord, the God of Abraham, Isaac and Jacob. I pray several times a day. I attend the synagogue on the Sabbath. Best of all, I know I am part of the worship and sacrifice in the Temple in Jerusalem, and I go whenever I can."

AD34

"Simon, tell us something about yourself and how you pray."
"First, let me say Jesus changed my name to Peter. I still pray several times a day. I attend the synagogue on the Sabbath. I know I am part of the worship in the Temple in Jerusalem and I go when I can. I also now pray 'Our Father', as Jesus taught us, and obey his command 'Do this in memory of me'. I used to think the Temple worship and sacrifice was the greatest prayer, but I'm beginning to wonder."

AD60

"Peter, tell us something about yourself and how you pray."
"I'm a follower of Jesus. I'm here in Rome to tell people the Good News. I pray several times each day, especially the prayer 'Our Father'. I am no longer welcome in the synagogue. I can no longer go to the Temple in Jerusalem, but day by day I am beginning to understand something amazing. All my needs to pray deeply and to offer sacrifice are satisfied by obeying Our Lord's command: 'Do this in memory of me.' All the sacrifices of the Temple, or any sacrifice, are only shadows of the sacrifice of Jesus which is here and now, and which we enter into when we do as he commanded."

Think back

Name the principal parts of the Mass. How does the celebration of Mass recall and represent what Jesus did?

Think and talk

How do Simon Peter's ways of praying change? What makes him change? What would he recognise in a celebration of Mass today? Every Eucharist is celebrated in obedience to Jesus' words "Do this in memory of me".

Michael, a twenty-first century Christian, writes:

"Being a Christian is important to me. I used to go to Mass with my parents, but I stopped going for nearly a year, because I got bored of the same thing every week. Then I went on a school retreat. It was a great experience. I understood why the Eucharist is so important. It's not just to receive Jesus in communion. It's just as important to be there and take part because it's sharing Jesus' love and sacrifice. There's a time in the Mass when the priest says:

'Through him, with him and in him, in the unity of the Holy Spirit, all glory and honour is yours, almighty Father, for ever and ever'. Everyone says 'Amen', that means 'yes'. I'm beginning to understand how I can't be a follower of Jesus without saying 'yes' to being part of his love and sacrifice, just like the disciples did 2,000 years ago."

1. What has Michael learned about the Eucharist?
2. How has this changed his attitude?
3. "I can't be a follower of Jesus without saying 'yes' to being part of his love and sacrifice." Why do you think this is important?

An everlasting covenant

The most important words in the celebration of the Eucharist are taken from the Last Supper, so it is important to understand what Jesus and his disciples were doing at that meal. Read Matthew 26:17–19.

The Jewish people were commanded to celebrate the Passover meal so that they would never forget that God had rescued them from the slavery of Egypt and led them to freedom in the Promised Land. In it they re-live this great moment of their history. They remember and celebrate God's faithfulness and the covenant in which they became God's People. As they blessed and ate bread and wine, they remembered how God had provided them with food and water in the desert.

Jesus made the connection between the covenant and what he was doing very clear for his disciples. Read Luke 22:14–20.

Find and write out the prayer 'Lamb of God' from the Mass.
Why is Jesus called the Lamb of God? (Hint: Exodus, Passover.)
What does this say about the sacrifice of Jesus?

2C Sacrifice

It is right to give God thanks and praise

1. Now study these extracts from one of the Church's Eucharistic prayers.

2. What do they tell you about the Church's faith and why the Eucharist is the greatest sacrament?

   Look for links to:

   – the Last Supper

   – the covenant

   – God's faithfulness

   – Jesus' death on the cross.

   Make notes.

3. Use ICT skills to produce a chart to show:

(a) how Peter came to understand the importance of what Jesus commanded

(b) what Michael learned about why the Eucharist was important

(c) words from the Eucharistic prayer that support your findings in (a) and (b).

1. Blessed are you, God of holiness:
   you accompany us with love
   as we journey through life.
   Blessed too is your Son, Jesus Christ,
   who is present among us
   and whose love gathers us together.
   As once he did for his disciples,
   Christ now opens the scriptures for us
   and breaks the bread.

2. Great and merciful Father, we ask you:
   send down your Holy Spirit
   to hallow these gifts of bread and wine,
   that they may become for us
   the body and blood of our Lord, Jesus Christ.

3. On the eve of his passion and death,
   while at table with those he loved,
   he took bread and gave you thanks:
   he broke the bread,
   gave it to his disciples, and said:
   Take this, all of you, and eat it:
   this is my body which will be given up for you.
   When supper was ended, he took the cup;
   again, he gave you thanks
   and, handing the cup to his disciples, he said:
   Take this, all of you, and drink from it:
   this is the cup of my blood,
   the blood of the new and everlasting covenant.
   It will be shed for you and for all so that sins
   may be forgiven.

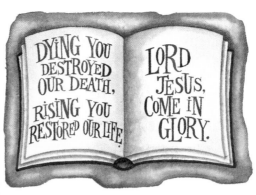

4. Let us proclaim the
   mystery of faith:
   When we eat this bread and drink this cup,
   we proclaim your death, Lord Jesus,
   until you come in glory.

5. And so, Father most holy,
   we celebrate the memory of Christ, your Son,
   whom you led through suffering
   and death on the cross
   to the glory of the resurrection
   and a place at your right hand.
   Until Jesus, our Saviour, comes again,
   we proclaim the work of your love
   and we offer you the bread of life
   and the cup of eternal blessing.

6. **The Eucharist prayer ends:**
   When our pilgrimage on earth is complete,
   welcome us into your heavenly home,
   where we shall dwell with you for ever.
   There, with Mary, the Virgin Mother of God,
   with the apostles, the martyrs,
   (Saint N) and all the saints,
   we shall praise you and give you glory
   through Jesus Christ, your Son.
   Through him,
   with him,
   in him,
   in the unity of the Holy Spirit,
   all glory and honour is yours,
   almighty Father,
   for ever and ever.
   Amen.

Alternative Eucharistic Acclamations

Christ has died.
Christ is risen.
Christ will come again.

Dying you destroyed our death,
rising you restored our life.
Lord Jesus, come in glory.

Lord, by your cross and resurrection you have set us free.
You are the Saviour of the world.

Bread and wine: body and blood

Bread and wine are symbols of human need for food and drink.
In the Bible they signify God's love and care.
Look up Genesis 1:29 and Exodus 16:14–15.
What do they show about God?

Now read these prayers over the gifts.
What is the same?
What is different?

> **Blessed are you, Lord, God of all creation.**
> **Through your goodness we have this bread to offer, which earth has given and human hands have made.**
> **It will become for us the bread of life.**

> **Blessed are you, Lord, God of all creation.**
> **Through your goodness we have this wine to offer, fruit of the vine and work of human hands.**
> **It will become for us our spiritual drink.**

Discuss

Look at the pictures of the wheat and vine.
What has to happen before the wheat becomes bread and the grapes become wine?
In what ways are these images of what happened to Jesus?
What do they say about the self-giving of Jesus?
Remember the image he used of the grain of wheat. (Check your memory, John 12:24.)

Another level

The bread and wine also symbolise the life and work of each person offered to God. What do you think people might be offering? In what ways are people's offerings joined to the offering of Jesus? (Hint: bread: body; wine: blood.)

Homework

Jesus says, "This is my body, given for you."

The Christian says, "This is my body, given for you."

Tell the story of someone you know or have heard about, in whose life the sacrifice of Jesus is reflected in great or small ways.

Extension

Write an entry for a Christian Handbook to explain the place and significance of bread and wine in the Sacrament of the Eucharist.

Reflect

Jesus is the only one who can say that his body and blood are the sacrifice that forgives the sins of the world.

Do this in memory of me

=== **Classwork** ===

The whole of the Eucharist is a response to Jesus' command "Do this in memory of me".

A. *Recall the actions of the Eucharist and match words to the rites. Use a missal or Mass sheet as additional resources to help you.*

Gathering rites

Liturgy of the Word

Profession of faith and procession with gifts

Liturgy of the Eucharist

Rite of Communion

Sending forth

B. *What does this say about the importance of the Eucharist for Catholics?*

Thinking about the following questions may help.

Is the Eucharist just about Mass on Sunday?

Does the Eucharist go beyond the doors of the church?

Where would you find these things happening in everyday life?

C. *Look at these words from John's gospel.*

I am the vine, you are the branches. Those who abide in me and I in them bear much fruit, because apart from me you can do nothing.
(John 15:5)

Those who love me will keep my word, and my Father will love them, and we will come to them and make our home in them. Whoever does not love me does not keep my words; and the word that you hear is not mine, but is from the Father who sent me.
(John 14:24)

I pray that they may all be one. Father! May they be in us, just as you are in me and I am in you. May they be one, so that the world will believe that you sent me.
(John 17:21)

This is my commandment, that you love one another just as I have loved you.
(John 15:12)

Learning together.

Living together.

The work of human hands.

Celebrating together.

What links can you make between the celebration of Eucharist and these words from John's gospel? Remember to look at images and symbols as well as words.

2C Sacrifice

Response

Glossary

Enter these words in your personal glossary with a brief explanation for each:

sacrifice
Lamb of God
memorial
communion
Do this in
  memory of me

Assessment ❓

1. *What were Jesus and his disciples celebrating at the last supper meal?*

2. *Write out the words and actions of Jesus at the last supper that are central to the Mass.*

3. *Choose one Eucharistic acclamation and explain it.*

4. *What is the Eucharist remembering?*

5. *What do Catholics believe about the Eucharist?*

Reflect

Jesus said: "If you eat my flesh and drink my blood you live in me and I in you."

Dilemma

Jesus said: "Whoever eats my flesh and drinks my blood lives in me, and I live in him." Some of his disciples found this too hard to take and they went away. What do you think?

Living faith

This is my body, broken for you,
bringing forgiveness, making you free.
Take it and eat it, and when you do,
do it in love for me.

This is my blood poured out for you,
bringing forgiveness, making you free.
Take it and drink it, and when you do,
do it in love for me.

'This is my body', Jimmy Owens

Go further

A satellite is being launched with a record of the world and its people. Write the text for a one-minute recording explaining the significance of the Sacrament of the Eucharist for Catholics.

Resurrection

In this section of our work we will be learning:

- about what makes people want to live
- that the Resurrection of Jesus is the heart of the Christian Faith
- about Catholic belief and teaching about death and resurrection.

If you saw a young child in this situation, what would you do? Why?

Do you think the person in the car is wearing a seatbelt just because it is the law? Could there be another reason?

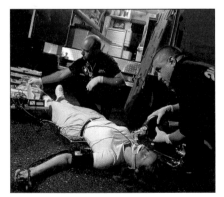

What is happening? What is the priority for the Emergency Services?

What theme do all the pictures have in common?

Record and discuss your answers.

Imagine this

Think of a time when you have almost hurt yourself badly. If you can't think of anything, imagine slipping on ice on your way to school or missing your footing on the stairs.

Replay the incident in slow motion in your mind. Were you aware of thinking about saving yourself, or did you just react automatically? Make a note of your thoughts on this and share them with someone else. Listen to their story.

What price a life?

It is a basic *instinct* in human beings to preserve our own lives and the lives of others. The power of this instinct is evident in people who put their own lives at risk for others, for example, giving a kidney to a relative.

Imagine being in a position where you have to choose whether to save yourself, a person you love, a stranger, or valuable possessions. Would you really have to think?

instinct: most natural response or action.

Some people put their lives at risk for the sake of money, power, status and success or adventure. Should the search for adventure and pushing yourself to the limit put the lives of others at risk? In groups, or with a partner, find examples of acceptable and unacceptable risks.

Sometimes a person loses the sense of value he or she has for their life. They may choose to commit suicide. When this happens we feel great sadness, and sense that there is something wrong in our world if this can happen. People say: "What a waste!" and "What could I have done?"

Discuss

What does this signify? What are people trying to do? What else might people do when sudden death(s) happens?

Time of death

2

Nothing is more certain in life than death. Everyone has to cope with it at some stage. Usually we have to face the death of a loved one before we have to come to terms with our own death. Bereavement, the death of someone you love, can be very difficult to deal with. It's hard to understand the different feelings it brings. It raises all sorts of difficult questions. It seems so impossible to make sense of, that we can begin to doubt things we have always believed. Although bereavement

can make some people have doubts about God, it can be something that makes a person turn to or return to their faith. They may do this both for comfort and to try to make sense of what has happened. One of the things people do when someone dies is send a card to the closest relatives of the deceased, the person who has died, offering sympathy.

Look at the messages on these cards. Additional material on *Copymaster* 12 :

On death and dying

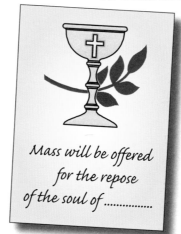

Design your own card and verse to send to a friend who has lost a close relative.

Reflect

And life is eternal and love is immortal, and death is only an horizon, and an horizon is nothing, save the limit of our sight.

(Bede Jarrett, OP, d 1934)

Think back

Her sorrow was turned into joy.
Tell the story.

Noli Me Tangere, Titian, 1511–12.

Rest in peace

You could say the Church began with a death! In fact, if it were not for the death of Jesus, Christianity wouldn't exist. The Church believes that Jesus' death was not an end, but a beginning. On the third day he rose again.

The last celebration for a Christian is a funeral Mass.
Read Ben's description of his feelings about his Grandfather's death.

"I couldn't believe it when Grandad died. I suppose I thought he'd live forever. In a way I was kind of glad that he wasn't in pain any more. I found the funeral quite difficult. I felt lots of different emotions. My eyes filled with tears when they brought his body into church and I turned round and saw how many people had come to pay their respects. I felt a lump in my throat when the priest was talking about what a wonderful man he had been. Looking back, I don't know if I felt like this because I was sad or because I was proud that I was so close to him. I had to smile when we sang his favourite hymn, 'Abide with me'. The words are quite sad, but I will always remember him at Mass singing it loudly, and not always in tune.

I laughed out loud at some of the things my dad said when he gave his speech. He said Grandad had excellent hearing when anyone asked him if he'd like a drink, but his hearing aid stopped working when he was told it was his turn to buy the drinks!

I found what the priest said about Grandad going to be with God very comforting. He said it was what Jesus promised. Thinking about that was the only way I could get my head round watching his coffin being lowered into the grave. I believe that he is with God and that he is somehow looking down and keeping an eye on me. I know that he would want me to look after Gran for him.

It's funny, but I enjoy coming to visit his grave. It's very peaceful, and although it might sound silly, I feel I can still talk to Grandad about the times we had together and about my problems. Sometimes I'd swear I can hear him crack one of his corny jokes and start chuckling."

1. Select from the following list the feelings Ben experienced when his Grandad died and during his funeral and burial:

> anger
> sadness
> happy memories
> jealousy
> humour
> wanting to laugh
> pride
> reassurance
> feeling comforted
> boredom
> worry
> faith in God

2. For each feeling you have chosen, give evidence from what Ben said.

3. Do you think it is inappropriate to have any of these feelings when a close relative has died? Give reasons for your answers.

4. Did you get the impression that Ben was trying not to break down in tears? What are your views on this?

5. What does Ben believe has happened to his Grandad now?

6. What do you think about Ben still talking to his Grandad in the graveyard?

Prayers from the Funeral Mass:
Copymaster 13

Find and read the Prayers of Farewell that end the funeral service. There are some lovely modern versions of the Antiphon 'May the angels lead you to paradise'. Find one and listen to it.

2D Resurrection

The Resurrection of Jesus

2

All that the Church believes about death and resurrection is founded on the resurrection of Jesus. It is at the centre of the whole of Christian faith. The gospel writers are in no doubt that Jesus died and was buried, and that he is risen and alive. The resurrection accounts are both confident and mysterious. Paul's letters are the earliest Christian writings. He proclaims the resurrection. He reminds the new Christians that he is ready to take risks because death is not the end.

Read the following passages.

◆ Source one: the burial of Jesus, Matthew 27:57–66.

◆ Source two: the Resurrection, John 20:1–10.

◆ Source three: the walk to Emmaus, Luke 24:13–35.

◆ Source four: Jesus appears to the Twelve (with and without Thomas), John 20:19–29.

◆ Source five: Paul writes to the Corinthians, 1 Corinthians 15:1–6, 19–20.

Classwork

A. Answer the following questions.

◆ *Source one: why were the Jewish leaders so keen for the Romans to put guards on Jesus' tomb?*
Do you think it likely that anyone could have stolen Jesus' body and 'invented' the Resurrection?

◆ *Source two: how do you think Mary Magdalene felt when she arrived at the tomb to discover that the stone had been rolled away from the entrance of the tomb?*
Have you any ideas about who 'the other disciple' might have been?

◆ *Source three: why do you think the two disciples didn't recognise Jesus?*
What made them recognise him in the end?

◆ *Source four: what made Thomas doubt that Jesus had risen when his friends told him what they had seen?*
What made him believe in the end?
What do you think Jesus meant by "Happy are those who believe without seeing me"?

◆ *Source five: what is Paul's message about the foundations for Christian faith?*
What hope does he offer the Corinthians?
What is common to all five sources?

B. *Using information from all five sources, imagine that you have to conduct an investigation into the disappearance of Jesus' body. This should include interviews with key witnesses and a presentation of the evidence. Prepare the questions for both interviews.*

C. *"The gospels do not explain the resurrection; the resurrection explains the gospels." What do you think this writer meant?*

Extension

1 ◆ Use the work you have done on the gospel accounts to prepare a dramatic presentation of the resurrection story. Perhaps you could role-play a court scene, present evidence on tape, write transcripts of interviews or present newspaper coverage of the incident. Or use music, mime and words.

2 ◆ *I believe! We believe!* Copymaster 14

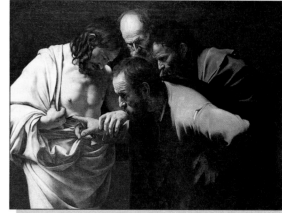

Doubting Thomas, Caravaggio, 1595–60.

Assessment

1. Christians believe in the resurrection of the body and the life of the world to come. Explain what this means.

2. The gospel writers record different resurrection stories:

   (a) According to Matthew's gospel, why would it have been difficult to steal Jesus' body?

   (b) In John's account of the empty tomb, which disciple entered the tomb first and found Jesus' body had gone?

   (c) What was the name of the disciple who wanted actual proof that Jesus had risen?

   (d) According to Luke's gospel, Jesus appeared to two disciples on the road to Emmaus. At first they did not recognise him. What eventually made them realise who he was?

3. Describe at least two different ways the gospel of the resurrection was received.

Living faith

Anne, a teacher who was dying of a terminal illness, wrote these words to be read to her friends and pupils at her funeral:

"I have no fear of death. I have not lived a blameless life, but I know that God has forgiven me for the mistakes I have made. I feel sorry that I cannot hold on to this life any longer, but I want to thank you for the love that you have shared with me, and the wealth and quality of emotions you have showered upon me in my life. Be good to each other, and remember that love is the only thing that can keep this world together. So goodbye, my friends, and rest assured that I will be seeing you again. God loves us too much to allow that not to happen."

Do you think Anne was a Christian? What evidence in her words can you find to support your view?

Would you imagine that hearing these words at the funeral helped her friends and pupils to deal with the sadness of her death? Explain your answer.

Dilemma

If the Church believes in 'Life after death', surely funerals should be joyful occasions.

Go further

"In the end, it is our understanding of death which decides our answers to all the questions that life puts to us." (Dag Hammarskjold)

"If a man hasn't discovered something he is willing to die for, he isn't fit to live." (Martin Luther King)

How do these sayings confirm, challenge and expand your ideas about death?

2D Resurrection

Something worth living for

Create a wall-size spider graph around 'Religion is ...'

What evidence do you see of positive and negative experiences of religion?

Agree a one-sentence explanation of 'Religion'.

Work in groups

Study the pictures.
1 What examples can you find in these photographs of the ideas in your spider graph?
2 What evidence can you find that religion:
   ◆ is important at different stages of life
   ◆ can have a positive influence
   ◆ can be a source of tension.
Share your findings.

In this section of our work we will be learning:

◆ about how religion affects people's lives
◆ about the Church's belief that Jesus is the way, the truth and the life
◆ about some tensions that exist between the gospel message and society today.

Siege at the Sikh Golden Temple, India.

A Bar Mitzvah celebration, Jerusalem.

Hindu funeral rites, India.

Reflect

How old is the idea of God?
Why is it world-wide throughout history?

Think back

Write one statement about Jesus that you have learned from the gospels. Begin your statement: 'Jesus is ...' Add these to your spider graph display.

A vandalised mosque in Kosovo.

A life for the world

The Church believes that, in Jesus, all human understanding about God is surpassed. Jesus makes it possible for all people, old and young and of all nations, to see and know the love, truth and life of God. The disciples who met him believed in him. They became witnesses. Through their faith and example, others heard the message and learned to believe. Read 1 John 1:1–5.

John's gospel has a series of statements in which Jesus uses images of himself and his mission.

I am the bread of life.
Whoever comes to me will never be hungry (John 6:35).

If anyone is thirsty let them come to me!
Whoever believes in me will never thirst (John 7:38).

I am the light of the world.
Anyone who follows me will not be walking in the dark, but will have the light of life (John 8:12).

I am the gate.
Anyone who enters through me will be safe (John 10:9).

I am the good shepherd.
I know my own and my own know me (John 10:14).

I am the resurrection.
Whoever lives and believes in me will never die (John 11:25).

> *I am the bread of life.*
>
> *I am the light of the world.*
>
> *I am the gate.*
>
> *I am the good shepherd.*
>
> *I am the resurrection.*
>
> As a class: brainstorm people whose faith in Jesus is recorded in the New Testament, in the gospels or letters. Which of the statements from John's gospel would each of them stand by?

Classwork ✍

A. Match the sayings with the following words. You may use words more than once.

safety	warmth	life
direction	direction	light
security	leadership	drink
shelter	protection	food

What does this say about Jesus and those who believe in him?

B. Choose one of John's statements. Find it in the gospel. Put the saying in its wider context. Who was Jesus talking to? What was he saying about himself and his mission?

C. In 2A you explored Jesus' question, "Who do you say I am?" and how important it is for each Christian to answer it personally. How would these statements help a Christian to answer Jesus' question? Present your answer in words and images. Use as sources one of the following: religious art, religious music.

Reflect

Witnesses spread the gospel, not words.

Homework 🏛

Choose one of these people. Imagine you are the person and write a letter to the Church of the twenty-first century. Explain how your faith in Jesus began. Suggest reasons why people should put their faith in Jesus.

The way, the truth and the life

Christians all over the world live by their faith in Jesus. Being a disciple is more than doing what Jesus said. Think back to the work you did on life as a pilgrimage with Jesus (1A). Jesus invites his disciples to a relationship so intimate that Jesus' way of living, the truth of his gospel and his life become the way of life, the truth and the life of the disciple. The third millennium is a time to ask how this Good News of Jesus and his invitation to communion is to be carried to all people.

In Jewish law the Jubilee was a celebration of God as Lord of all the earth and of all people. The sound of a horn announced the beginning of the Great Jubilee. *Yobel* is Hebrew for 'horn', from which we get the English word 'jubilee'.

The celebration took place every 50 years. The Jubilee called people:

- to walk in freedom: slaves were to be returned to their families
- to do justice: land was to be returned to rightful owners
- to recognise life as God's gift: instead of the labour of sowing and reaping, people would eat what the land produced naturally.

The Church celebrated the year 2000 as a Great Jubilee and invited all believers to carry this idea into a new millennium.

Study the words of this song, especially written for Jubilee 2000.

Verse 1
We are young, we are old,
in your world our lives unfold.
All around us earth's abundance
brings more than our hand can hold.
Set us free. Make us see what our
stewardship must be:
all the gifts of your creation shared out equally.

Refrain
Let the trumpet sound to announce the year.
Let it tell God's people that their time is here.
Like a living stream, let mercy flow.
Like a mountain high, let justice grow.
Let the reign of God from sea to sea
set captives free.
Cry "Jubilee!"

Verse 2
For the sake of the poor
Jesus came and gladly bore condemnation and derision from those who enshrined 'the law'.
He proclaimed endlessly laws of love and jubilee, breaking chains of debt and empire, setting nations free.

Verse 3
All the land, soil and seed, can provide
for ev'ry need.
Yet God's children thirst and hunger,
divided by human greed.
Let the earth, sea and sky, now reflect and glorify God, whose tenderness and mercy lift
the lowly high.

Verse 4
Jesus Christ yesterday and tomorrow
and today, through all times and through all ages, your word is our living way.
That the world be made new, keep your gospel people true.
Let us once again with courage rise and follow you.

'Jubilee Song', Bernadette Farrell
(for CAFOD)

Live Jubilee

Listen to and sing the Jubilee Song.

Work in groups. Using the words of the song, identify ways in which Jesus and his gospel offer the world the way, truth and life.

It may help you to ask what the song has to say about:

- relationships between people and God, between individuals and nations
- the relationship between people and creation
- justice and truth, honesty and fair dealing
- Jesus and his message.

Discuss

How could Jubilee become an experience in the life of:

- a young person
- an older person.

In today's world, how might the aims of the Jubilee:

- clash with values and attitudes
- bring hope.

Class project

Witnesses in every walk of life

Collect evidence of people for whom their faith in Jesus is important and put together a class 'Record of Witnesses'.

Your record can be made up of words, music, pictures, recordings and other media.

Your witnesses can come from the present day or from history.

They can be famous people or members of your family or friends.

Agree the criteria you will use to decide whom to choose.

Use at least two of the following resources: a dictionary of biography, life stories (for example, *Faith in Action* series), a TV religious programme.

1. Prepare a statement of not more than 30 words to explain why the person you have chosen should be included in the Record.

   Use *Copymaster* 15 as a model: ***Model for a witness profile***

2. Listen to the statements and put together your Record.

Reflect

How could Jubilee become an experience in your life?

Jubilee icons from Turvey Abbey, Bedfordshire.

Response

Reflect

When nations and individuals are in deep trouble we look for a way out.

Philosophy says: think your way out.

Science says: invent your way out.

Business says: work your way out.

Armies say: fight your way out.

Religion says: pray your way out.

Jesus says: I am the way.

(Source unknown)

Assessment ?

1. *Give four of Jesus' "I am" statements from John's gospel.*

2. *Explain the biblical meaning of 'jubilee'.*

3. *Select words and phrases from the Jubilee Song that show the true meaning of Jubilee.*

4. *What phrase from John's gospel shows that being a Christian without Jesus is impossible?*

5. *Choose someone from the class 'Record of Witnesses' and explain what makes them a good witness. (Not your own.)*

Glossary

Enter these words in your personal glossary with a brief explanation for each:

Jubilee
witness
society
God

Dilemma

Christianity is a statement which, if false, is of no importance, and, if true, is of infinite importance. The one thing it cannot be is moderately important. (C S Lewis)

Can you take the risk?

Living faith

One more step along the world I go,
one more step along the world I go;
from the old things to the new,
keep me travelling along with you.

And it's from the old I travel to the new;
keep me travelling along with you.

Round the corner of the world I turn,
more and more about the world I learn;
all the new things that I see,
you'll be looking at along with me.

As I travel through the bad and good,
keep me travelling the way I should;
where I see no way to go,
you'll be telling me the way, I know.

Give me courage when the world is rough,
keep me loving though the world is tough;
leap and sing in all I do,
keep me travelling along with you.

You are older than the world can be,
you are younger than the life in me;
ever old and ever new,
keep me travelling along with you.

'One more step', Sidney Carter

What do you think Christians, young and old, find encouraging in this song?

Go further

Choose one current film or TV show you have seen.
What, if any, tensions does it show between the Gospel message and society today?
Write to a radio or TV 'points of view' programme, giving your opinion as a Christian.

Other faiths: Islam

Think back

How does learning about other people's faith help you, the school community, society, the world?

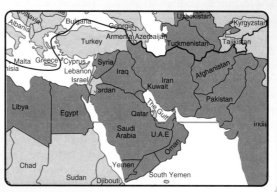

In this section of our work we will be learning:

- something of the beginnings of Islam and Muhammad its founder
- about the five duties (Pillars) of Islam.

Fact file:

Islam means 'submission to God'.

Islam is the religion of submission to the one God.

It has its roots in the north-west part of Arabia in the seventh century.

It spread north into Palestine and Syria, Iraq and Iran and into Central Asia, and next to Egypt, Morocco, Spain and Portugal. Use an atlas to find the most populous Islamic countries today: the Arab Middle East, Indonesia, Pakistan, Bangladesh and India.

Today there are about 1.5 million Muslims in Britain.

Islam's founder, Muhammad, was born in Mecca in AD570.

His parents died when he was young and relatives brought him up.

During the course of his life he had some striking religious experiences.

He said he saw the angel Gabriel, who made him read from a book, and told him about the will of Allah; he felt certain words in his heart, which he took to be from God. Over a period of 23 years he, and later his followers, collected all these words in what is now known as the Qur'an, the Holy Book of Islam. The word *Qur'an* means 'that which is read'. It is written in Arabic.

During some of his religious experiences he felt he was transported to Jerusalem, to the Temple Mount. He saw Abraham, Moses and Jesus, and he received instructions about how people should pray.

To Muslims, the Qur'an is not simply a holy book like many others.
It is the divine thought and words of God.
Muhammad is the prophet of God.
For Muslims he is the final prophet.
He died in AD632.

- Research the Muslim population in Britain and the diversity of cultures Muslims come from. Find out: where do large Muslim communities live in Britain; where do Muslim pupils go to school; at least three cities that have mosques.
- Find out about a mosque: the design, how it is used, what people have to do before they enter, how they prepare for prayer: physically, spiritually, the actions of prayer. You may be able to visit a mosque; if not, try to watch a video or find a book in the library.

The Declaration of Faith: Shahadah

*There is no god but Allah
and Muhammad is the Messenger of Allah.*

A central belief for Muslims is faith in Allah, the One and only God. Islam does not allow any pictures or statues of Allah to be drawn or made, so that nothing can possibly distract from him. Muslim artists have, however, illustrated the names of Allah in beautiful ways. These names describe the qualities of Allah and are used to praise Him. There are 99 names of Allah. Below is a list of some of these.

The Compassionate   The Life-Giver
The Generous   The Hidden
The Friend   The Watcher
The Light   The Judge
The Avenger   The Forgiver
The Peace   The Just

Homework 🏛

Choose one of these names for Allah.

List some of the things it suggests about Allah.

Why do you think a Muslim might use this name, and when?

Illustrate the name.

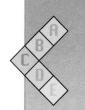

The Five Pillars of Islam

There are five duties for a follower of Islam. They are the marks of a believer, no matter where he or she lives throughout the world. This is what all Muslims believe Allah wants of them. They must:

Witness: Shahadah

Muslims must witness that there is no God but Allah and Muhammad is his Messenger: the Shahadah. When someone wants to become a Muslim they must make this declaration. It is said every time a Muslim prays. It helps believers to remember the greatness of Allah and all that he has done. Because Allah is so great the only possible response to Him is submission.

Pray: Salat

This is a way of communicating with Allah. There are important preparations for prayer. Muslims pray five times a day: the time for prayer is regulated by the sun, and the preparations for prayer all help to teach about people's relationship with Allah.

Fast: Sawm

During the month of Ramadam, Muslims fast from sunrise to sunset. The fast is the opportunity to practise sacrifice, self-discipline and patience.

Give alms: Zakat

Muslims must give a percentage (2.5 per cent) of savings every year to help the poor and needy. It is not just about doing good and being generous because one has plenty; it is about giving because Allah calls people to share.

Make pilgrimage: Hajj

Every Muslim must try to make a Pilgrimage to Makka, (Mecca) at least once in a lifetime. Makka is the birthplace of Muhammad and the site of the Ka'ba, the first house of God built on earth. Hajj takes place annually and Muslims who are healthy and can afford it are expected to go once in their lifetime.

Classwork

A. *As a class: watch a video about* Hajj.

1. *Make a note of the religious duties a Muslim has to perform when making* Hajj.
2. *Prepare a diary to be kept for each day of the* Hajj. *Give each day a heading.*
3. *Make a* Hajj *word list and explain the meaning of the words.*

B. *Work with a partner. Choose one of the Five Pillars. Visit the library or use the Internet to help you prepare a display for the classroom explaining the importance of the Pillar you have chosen. What is the duty? What does it teach about Allah? Before putting up your display, present it to the class.*

C. *Prepare a Year 7 Assembly on one of the Five Pillars, keeping in mind the time of the year and how appropriate it is. You will want to explain to Year 7 the importance of respecting the religious practices of others and of learning about them and from them.*

Reflect

What would identify a person as a believer?

Response

Reflect

Which of the Five Pillars would you find it most interesting or most challenging to do?

What activity of yours gives you the same feeling of sharing the life of a community?

Reflect

Glossary

Enter these words in your personal glossary with a brief explanation for each:

Shahadah
the Five Pillars of Islam
the *Qu'ran*
Muhammad
Mecca

Friday service in a Bradford mosque.

Assessment

1. *Name the Five Pillars of Islam.*
2. *Describe one feature of Muslim prayer.*
3. *Who was the Prophet Muhammad?*
4. *What is the Qur'an?*
5. *Name one of the duties Muslims must perform during the Hajj.*

Reflect

None of you truly believes until he wishes for his brother what he wishes for himself.

From the *Hadith*, the sayings of the Prophet Muhammad

Reflect

Dilemma

'Submission to God.' How can this lead to freedom?

Final thought

What do you truly believe?

The common good

What makes a team member?
Imagine you are going to form a new team for a sport, hobby, project or play.
Study the criteria below.

The team member must:

(a) share the goals of the team
(b) be willing to make sacrifices
(c) recognise and respond to the needs of others
(d) be able to work independently
(e) have a good sense of humour
(f) have skills and training relevant to the task
(g) be flexible
(h) not embarrass the team by confrontational behaviour
(i) show dedication and commitment at all times
(j) be thick-skinned
(k) have a good personality and social skills
(l) be assertive in stating his/her opinions
(m) have a strong sense of fairness for all
(n) show a commitment to raising the achievement of less able team members
(o) believe in him/herself.

Which criteria would you use to select your team members?

Rank the criteria on a scale of one to three, where one is the most suitable and three is the least suitable.

With a partner, discuss:
◆ what qualities are required for team membership?
◆ what qualities could harm the team spirit?
◆ what choices does a team manager have when a team member stops working for the benefit of others and instead works selfishly?

Try to come up with some examples of this.

Reflect

It's the playing together that makes the sound what it is, a symphony.

In this section of our work we will be learning:

◆ about the challenge to balance personal needs and the common good
◆ how Jesus' teaching challenges Christians to work for the common good.

I'M ALL RIGHT, JACK
It's not fair
WHO CARES
You've got to look after yourself
WHAT'S IN IT FOR ME?

As a class, discuss:

how many of the graffitti sayings are you familiar with? How frequently do you hear them? Where? When? On what occasions?

Work in groups. Choose one of the sayings.

Work out a situation when it was used.

Role-play the two sides of the argument.

Evaluate

What did we learn from the role-play, from looking at both sides?

Think back

Name and explain, using words or pictures, three New Testament images that illustrate the closeness of Jesus and the Church.
(Hint: John 15:1; 1 Corinthians 12:12.)

Let justice flow

3

Jesus is very sharp with those who think they can hide from their responsibilities towards the less fortunate. He calls them hypocrites, because they believe themselves to be good and do not care about others.

Jesus warns people that there will be a day of reckoning. Matthew's gospel records the parable of the last judgement. Its message is clear. At the end, people will be judged on how they have shown love, support, help – a sense of social responsibility – to their neighbour. Jesus identifies so closely with the less fortunate that he considers what has been done to them as having been done to him.

Read Matthew 25:31–46, the parable of the sheep and goats, and Luke 16:19–31, the parable of Dives and Lazarus.

"If only I had known!" Known what?
Answer this question on behalf of:
   – the sheep
   – the goats
   – Dives
   – Lazarus.

Being a brother or sister to others

The parable of the sheep and the goats describes the moment of judgement that the Church believes will come for each person and for the whole world. It points to the fact that heaven and hell are the results of the choices people make in the time and space of this life.

Their attitude and treatment of others is what separates the 'sheep' and 'goats'. Love equals justice.

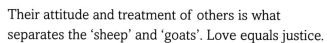

Discuss what justice means.
Is it all or some of the following?

being fair   *telling the truth*
keeping promises   *keeping the law*
respecting others   *getting your rights*
being responsible   *getting what you deserve*
doing good to others *paying a fair price*
punishing wrong-doers *praising/rewarding*
caring for the earth   *honest efforts*
                      earning a profit for
                          work done

≡ **Homework** ≡

Look through the local papers over a period of three or four days. Make a list and some notes of all the stories where people are fighting for some kind of justice.

Write a letter to the editor, for publication, commenting on one of these stories from a Christian perspective.

Not the end

Brainstorm:

Heaven is ...

Hell is ...

At the end of the world ...

What did you agree about?

What differences of opinion did you have? In what ways does the illustration reflect your views?

Science and religion agree that the world as we know it will end. Science has a number of theories, and even more questions, about how this might happen. Throughout history people have predicted the end. Groups have been known to give a date and make careful preparations for the final moments. So far, none of these predictions have come true.

The gospels record Jesus' warning not to waste time on this. Exactly what will happen and what will follow, no one knows except God the Father. All that is certain is that each person will die and at some time there will be an ending. What this life after death will be like depends on the choices we make in life.

The Church teaches about four last things: death, judgement, heaven and hell.

Traditional images of heaven and hell.

The most difficult aspect to get hold of in all this is that time and space, as we know them, will end.

Can you imagine life without time or space?

Have you ever lost your sense of time because you have been so completely taken up with what you are doing?

Perhaps this gives a small clue about what life for ever will be.

Neither heaven nor hell is a geographical place. You don't go there in a physical way.

Heaven is life in God: the joy and utter contentment of being with the One who is love and happiness for ever.

Hell is being separated from that same life, joy, happiness and presence.

◆ Read and role-play:

The rich man and Lazarus (Luke 16:9–31).

◆ Discuss (a) the imagery and (b) Jesus' teaching. How are both present in the way people talk about and think of heaven and hell today?

Info box

Purgatory is not a place. It is outside time and space. It expresses the Church's belief that people who have died might need to be freed from whatever would prevent them seeing and sharing the full beauty of God. It is a state of 'separating from' and 'making ready for'. The Church encourages everyone to pray for the dead, especially in the month of November.

3A The common good

A. *Look at the people listed.*

homeless man
unmarried pregnant teenager
man imprisoned for child abuse
malnourished child
person with HIV
victim of racial abuse
unemployed person
woman in exile from her own country
woman committed to God
man in public office

Draw up two lists entitled 'Least' and 'Most'.
Which cases are most likely to get media
coverage (TV and press)?
Which cases are least likely to get media
coverage?
Which cases are most likely to get support through a Church organisation?
Which cases are least likely to get support through a Church organisation?
Which cases are most likely to get support out of your pocket?
Which cases are least likely to get support out of your pocket?

Look back to your three answers under the 'least' likely questions.
What evidence do you have to support this?
What did Jesus say about the 'least' of our neighbours?

B. *What challenge does the parable of the sheep and the goats make*
to developing a sense of social responsibility:
in society
in the Church
in your school
in yourself?
Write an Action Plan outlining the steps you would take to try to develop
a sense of social responsibility in one of the above situations.

C. *With a partner, prepare a position statement (For or Against) to debate the*
following motion:
Am I my brother's/sister's keeper?
To help you in the task, read Genesis 4: 1–11.

Love in action

The Church takes very seriously Jesus' teaching about love of neighbour and care for others, especially those in need. It is more than 'doing good'. It recognises that each person is created by God. Each one's dignity comes from God and each one is to be treated with respect. This means working for the common good of all people.

Class task

As a class, take part in a CAFOD game: Are you on the sidelines? *Copymaster* 16

Who helps?

How many of the following agencies are likely to be able to provide help for some of the people in your 'least/most' lists? Choose as many organisations as you wish for each answer.

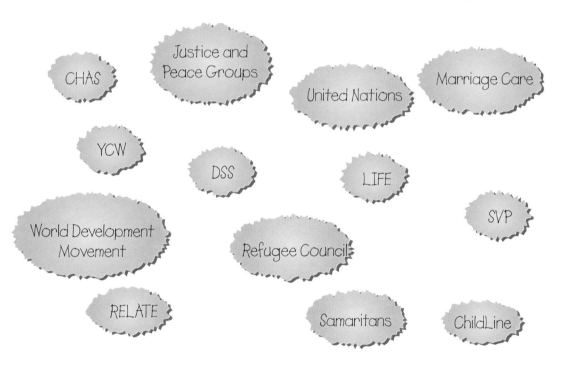

Make a list of the social issues the Catholic Church is working on in our world today through some of these agencies.

What does this say about the Church's understanding of Jesus' command to "love your neighbour as yourself"? Research the work of one of these agencies. Decide how you will present your findings to the class.

Reflect

Can Christians possibly say "It's not my problem"?

Reflect

Response

Reflect

The following verse is from a hymn that was popular in the last few hundred years:

The rich man in his castle,

The poor man at his gate,

The Lord God created them

And established their estate.

estate: position in life; class

Reflect

Discuss

What religious belief does this verse state accurately? What assumption is it making? Why might it cause problems for Christians today?

Dilemma

Complete the following sentences:

Faith without action ...

Action without faith ...

Living faith

The Lord hears the cry of the poor.

Blessed be the Lord.

Assessment ?

1. *What does the term 'the common good' mean for Christians?*
2. *Name one parable that tells of a judgement at the end of time.*
3. *What are 'the four last things'?*
4. *Define what it means to be 'just'.*
5. *'The least of my brothers and sisters' are ... who?*

Go further

Plan and put into practice a poster campaign for the school on 'The Common Good'. Include information about the Church's teaching and ideas for applying it in the school community and neighbourhood.

Glossary

Enter these words in your personal glossary with a brief explanation for each:

**the common good
justice
Catholic social
  action
the final
  judgement
complacency**

Living powerful lives

In this section of our work we will be learning:

◆ about attitudes to power and freedom
◆ about the power of the Holy Spirit
◆ about authority in the Church.

School power

Who are the powerful people in your school? Think about the roles of the headteacher, the deputies, the governors, parents, pupils, teaching and non-teaching staff.

1. Put together a profile of power in school.
2. Think about which people have power and how they use it. Is power always used for the good of the school community?
3. Present your ideas in a diagram.

Power talk

Advertising can be very powerful. This is why companies spend so much money on it. Many advertisers try to connect their products with powerful images and powerful-looking people. Many present their products as the way to freedom.

1. Do a survey of adverts on TV, in magazines, on billboards and so on.
2. What symbols of power do they present?
3. What kinds of power are being made to look attractive?
4. In what ways do these ideas of power appeal or not appeal to young people?
5. Does advertising set people free to stop and think?

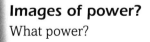

Images of power?
What power?

Power first

3 Read Junior's story and answer the questions at the end.

Junior was delighted. His mum had asked him to baby-sit on Saturday for a whole evening. He had looked after his younger sister and brother for an hour or two whilst his mum went to the shops, but he had never been left in charge for longer, and never at night! He thought of all the things he could do. He decided that he would get Carly and Jordan to bed as soon as possible and then entertain himself with his music collection, videos and computer games, stopping from time to time to raid the fridge.

When Saturday finally arrived Junior could hardly wait for the evening to come. It was about time that he had some time and space to himself. It seemed sometimes that Carly and Jordan came first, and that, because he was so much older, he had to be the one to make sacrifices. Tonight, though, would be for him, and he intended to make the most of it.

As his mum left the house, she kissed the children goodnight and told them that Junior was in charge. She then spoke very seriously to Junior about his responsibilities. She wrote down the phone number of the restaurant and made him promise to call her if anything happened. Junior promised, and when his mum said she wouldn't be late, he called after her that she could be as late as she wanted!

As the oldest in the house, the one in charge, Junior felt on top of the world. It was a wonderful feeling to have the power to control not only what he did, but also what two others would be allowed to do. The children wanted him to play with them and he gave them rides up and down the room pretending he was a racing car and they were Formula One drivers. They persuaded him to let them watch half an hour's TV, and read them a story. By the time Carly and Jordan were settled in bed Junior was exhausted, and felt tempted by sleep himself. But he did not want to miss this opportunity, so downstairs he went.

He was just deciding what to do first when the phone rang. It was Billy. He wanted to come round with the others from school. Junior immediately wished he hadn't mentioned the baby-sitting at school. There were five of them – including Simone! They had some cider and were ready to party. Junior had a problem. What Billy had in mind was certainly tempting ... but what would his mum say? Billy said that she'd never know, but Junior wasn't so sure. Anyway, he realised that even if mum didn't find out, he would know that he'd broken his promise and let her, Carly and Jordan down.

1. Why was Junior so pleased when he was asked to baby-sit?
2. What do you think Junior's mum said when she reminded him of his responsibilities?
3. Why did Junior delay putting the younger children to bed?
4. Why was Junior tempted by Billy's suggestion?
5. Write your own version of the end of the story.

As a class, recall the story of what happened at Pentecost.

The gift of power

Cardinals

Archbishops

Pope

Bishops

Lay People

Parish Priests

Discuss

People outside the Church see it as a world-wide organisation that, like any big organisation, needs people to keep everything working.

Who do you think are powerful people in the Church? How do they use their power?

The Church has a different ideal of power from business. Jesus promised his disciples power 'from on high'. This is God's power, given in the gift of the Holy Spirit. It is power given for the sake of others. Each Christian is baptised and confirmed in the power of the Holy Spirit to live the Christian life worshipping God and serving others. The gift of the Holy Spirit consecrates bishops and priests to the service of God in the Church. They are ministers of the gospel and the sacraments. By the power of the Spirit they teach and lead God's people.

We get a clue in the word the Church uses about power. It is 'authority' and comes from a Latin word *augere*, meaning 'to cause to grow'. Those who have authority in the Church have a duty to do all they can to help people to grow by responding to the gift of the Holy Spirit.

Through the centuries this ideal has not always been reached. Some churchmen have abused the power entrusted to them, but even this can be a sign of the power of the Holy Spirit. In spite of human weakness, the Church has continued to proclaim the gospel and hold up the ideal.

The gift of authority

The Church believes that the Holy Spirit has always guided its leaders. The power and authority that is the gift of the Holy Spirit has been passed down from the apostles, led by Peter, to the Pope and Bishops today. Together they form the *Magisterium* of the Church, from the Latin word meaning 'teaching'. When there are important matters of teaching to decide, the Pope and Bishops meet in General Council. The Church believes that the Holy Spirit guides their decisions in a special way.

The Church throughout the world is divided into dioceses.

These are texts from the rite of ordination for a bishop:

The Bishop has the responsibility to exercise leadership on behalf of the Church in the diocese. A diocese can cover a very large area and is divided into parishes and deaneries, groups of parishes, to make it easier to manage, create the sense of a parish family and help people to feel part of the wider Church community.

Prostration during the Litany of the Saints.

As a father and a brother, love all those whom God places in your care. Love the priests and deacons who share with you the ministry of Christ. Love the poor and infirm, strangers and the homeless. Encourage the faithful to work with you in your apostolic task; listen willingly to what they have to say. Never relax your concern for those who do not yet belong to the one fold of Christ; they too are commended to you in the Lord. Never forget that in the Catholic Church, made one by the bond of Christian love, you are incorporated into the *college of bishops*. You therefore should have a constant concern for all the churches and gladly come to the aid and support of churches in need.

Classwork

A. Look at the words spoken to a bishop at his ordination. What advice is he given about serving the people of his diocese? Many bishops have a motto. Create one, using ideas from the texts you have read.

B. Jesus calls his followers to service. Identify the ways a bishop is called to use the authority he is given for the good of (a) his diocese; (b) the whole Church. Using the title 'Remember this', write five points to help a new bishop remember the words of his ordination day.

C. One of the Pope's titles is 'Servant of the Servants of God'. Research some of the things the present Pope has said and done that reflect this title.

The laying on of hands.

Pentecost every day

Each year at Pentecost the Church celebrates the power of the Spirit at work in the whole Church and each and every member. Pentecost is the beginning of Ordinary Time in the Church's year. This tells us that the gift of the Spirit is not a 'one-off'. The Holy Spirit is alive and active throughout the year, every year, in the life and work of the whole Church.

Welsh Diocesan Youth Group at Lourdes.

Homework 🏛

Research into how your diocese is organised.

How are the gifts of the Spirit recognised and used for the good of the whole Church?

Think back to work you did in Year 7 on parish and diocese and what you learned about Confirmation in Year 8.

Try to include some of the following words:

The children's choir at Wrexham, Wales.

> laity
> deanery
> parish
> priest
> deacon
> Episcopal Vicar
> Dean
> Vicar General
> Bishop's council
> diocesan and parish
>   organisations

Millennium Youth Mass, Westminster.

Useful sources: Diocesan Directory, diocesan website, diocesan newspapers

Reflect

The Church is not just bishops and priests. Cardinal Newman once remarked that the Church would look very foolish without the laity.

Youth Gather, Arundel and Brighton.

3B Living powerful lives

Response

Reflect

What do you think of the idea that the only good use of power is power used for the service of others? What would this mean for
(a) the Prime Minister   (b) a religious leader?

tɔɘℲɘЯ

Assessment ?

1. *What symbolic action signifies the passing on of the power of the Spirit in the Church?*

2. *Which Sacraments celebrate this?*

3. *Give two examples of the power of the Holy Spirit at work in the apostles at Pentecost.*

4. *What is the Magisterium?*

5. *Name five different ways in which people exercise power and responsibility in the Church today.*

Living faith

In Scripture, Wisdom, working with God before creation, is named 'she'. This hymn for the Holy Spirit uses feminine imagery to sing of the work of the Holy Spirit from the beginning.

She sits like a bird, brooding on the waters,
hov'ring on the chaos of the world's first day;
she sighs and she sings, mothering creation,
waiting to give birth to all the Word will say.

She wings over earth, resting where she wishes,
lighting close at hand or soaring through the skies;
she nests in the womb, welcoming each wonder,
nourishing potential hidden to our eyes.

She dances in fire, startling her spectators,
waking tongues of ecstasy where dumbness reigned;
she weans and inspires all whose hearts are open,
nor can she be captured, silenced or restrained.

For she is the Spirit, one with God in essence,
gifted by the Saviour in eternal love;
she is the key opening the scriptures,
enemy of apathy and heavenly dove.

John L Bell and Graham Maule, from 'Enemy of Apathy', *Wild Goose Songs*, Volume 21, ©WGRG, The Iona Community

---

Glossary

Enter these words in your personal glossary with a brief explanation for each:

inspired
catechist
deanery
deacon
Trinity

Reflect

"...Send your Spirit upon these gifts, so that they may become for us the body and blood of your only Son Our Lord, Jesus Christ."

"Come, Holy Spirit, fill the hearts of your faithful and kindle in them the fire of your love."

tɔɘℲɘЯ

Dilemma

"No one can say 'Jesus is Lord' except by the Holy Spirit." Is it enough for a person to claim that he or she is led by the Holy Spirit?

Go further

Use your Bible skills to follow up the Scripture reference in the hymn. (Hints: Genesis, Annunciation, Pentecost, Nicodemus.)

Living commitment

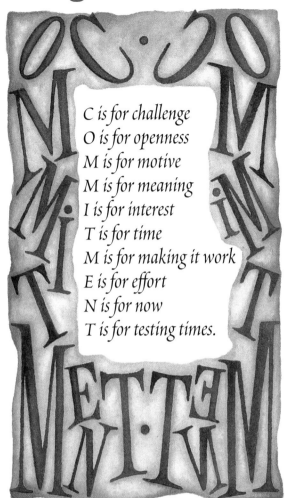

C is for challenge
O is for openness
M is for motive
M is for meaning
I is for interest
T is for time
M is for making it work
E is for effort
N is for now
T is for testing times.

In this section of our work we will be learning:

◆ about attitudes to commitment in the world today
◆ about Marriage and Holy Orders, sacraments for service.

Discuss

1. Show how all these are part of a commitment to
   – a relationship
   – a career path
   – a way of life

2. Use your own experience, stories of your friends or family, or from TV and the media to collect evidence of how these qualities affect commitment.

committed
single–minded
focused
obsessed
goal–orientated
determined
ruthless
ambitious
dedicated

Words we use

Study the words opposite. What attitudes towards commitment are reflected in them? Add any words you can.

Short term, long term

With a partner or in a group, discuss:

1. Which of the following might people see as short term commitments and which might be for life?

   school   marriage
   drama production   paper round
   religious life   caring for a pet
   a family   friendship

2. Add your own ideas.
3. Which will involve co-operation with others?
4. Name some people who you think show commitment.
5. What would life be like for you and others without their commitment?

Reflect

Where would we be without stickability?

Celebrating commitment

Every kind of commitment involves others at some point and in different ways. The Catholic Church celebrates two sacraments of service to the community, Marriage and Holy Orders. Each involves a lifelong commitment that signifies God's unshakeable commitment to human persons. Each sacrament deepens the relationship with God that began in baptism. These sacraments consecrate, that is, make holy, the love and self-giving of the wife and husband and the ordained priest so that they become signs of Christian love and self-giving for the whole Church.

Think back

What is a sacrament?

Marriage

A wedding is a day; a marriage is a lifetime.

1. Discuss what this means.
2. Make your own list of what marriage is about. This will include positive and negative aspects.
3. Study the prayers from the rite of marriage, *Copymaster* 17. Match the photos to the prayers.

The marriage vows.

The blessing and giving of rings.

Signing the Register.

Work as a class

1. Using the text of the prayers, identify the commitments the couple make. Make notes.
2. In what ways are these commitments service of others?
3. What are the symbols of commitment used in the marriage service?
4. What do they signify?
5. How do the prayers show that the sacrament of marriage reveals God's love?
6. Where is there recognition that life together is about good times and bad?
7. What are some of the challenges a couple might have to face in today's world?

Classwork

A. Work in groups of all boys and all girls. Identify what you would put in each suitcase for a successful lifelong marriage. Feedback to the other groups. Notice the similarities and differences between the sexes.

B. Re-read the prayers of the Catholic marriage service. What do they tell you about the Church's teaching on Christian marriage? List as points.
Compare these to the contents of your suitcase and discuss: what is the same and what is added?

C. What values and attitudes in society today can make it difficult for young people to commit themselves to one another in marriage? Use young people's magazines as your key source of evidence. Present your findings to the class.

3C Living commitment

Holy Orders

1. Write a job description for a priest.

2. If possible, invite a priest to discuss your ideas.

3. If possible, watch a video of an ordination.

4. From the video or the pictures on this page, identify the symbols used in the service.

Study the *Copymaster* 18 : ***Prayers from the Rites of Ordination***

Laying on of hands by the Bishop.

Candidates with their families.

Questions and promises.

The prostration.

The laying on of hands.

Families help the candidates with their vestments.

The anointing of hands.

The gifts of bread and wine.

The kiss of peace.

1. Select words from the prayers of ordination that describe
(a) the vocation of the priest – God's call for him
(b) what God wants him to do in response to this call
(c) the commitments the priest makes. These words may help you:

to serve	to lead
to teach	to pray
to care	to celebrate
to make holy	to give good example
to love	to be faithful
to proclaim	to offer sacrifice
holiness	to love wisdom
closeness to Christ	

2. What do you think might bring happiness and challenge in a priest's service of God and the Christian community? Make notes.

Homework 🏛

Use the words you have selected and the notes you made.

1. *Imagine you are a priest facing each of the following situations. What would you find rewarding? What would you find unrewarding? Grade your answers on a scale of one to five where one is unrewarding and five is very rewarding.*

    (a) *A small group in the parish wants the priest to meet and pray with them to help them grow in their faith.*

    (b) *A very sick man, dying of cancer, wants the priest to visit him regularly.*

    (c) *All the parish groups and organisations want the priest to chair all their meetings.*

    (d) *An engaged couple needs help preparing for marriage.*

    (e) *Parents of a young boy in trouble with the police want the priest to sort him out.*

2. *Write a brief paragraph naming the qualities that the priest would need to deal with these situations. Give reasons for your answer.*

3. *From the work you have done, what would you list as the number one, two and three duties and responsibilities of a priest?*

4. *How might a parish priest share some of his responsibilities and duties with lay men and women in the parish?*

5. *What difference would this make to the priest and the parish? (Think back to the work on the parish in Year 7.)*

Questioning commitment

70 per cent of people choose to live together rather than get married

Church Crisis: Vocations to the Priesthood Fall

Today it is sometimes easier to get people to commit themselves to a cause than to God and to another person. Why?

In what ways do you think the Church could encourage and support commitment to marriage and the priesthood?

3C Living commitment

Glossary

Enter these words in your personal glossary with a brief explanation for each:

commitment
marriage
holy orders

Assessment ⟨?⟩

1. What are the symbols used in the celebration of the Sacrament of Marriage?
2. Name two symbols used in the celebration of the Sacrament of Holy Orders.
3. What vows are taken in the marriage ceremony?
4. What promises are made in the ordination ceremony?
5. How do these sacraments reflect God's commitment?

Reflect

Read 1 Corinthians 13.
Is this description of love timeless?

Dilemma

Is anything for ever?

Living faith

> Will you let me be your servant?
> Let me be as Christ to you;
> Pray that I may have the grace to
> Let you be my servant, too.
>
> We are pilgrims on a journey,
> We are travellers on the road;
> We are here to help each other
> Walk the mile and bear the load.
>
> I will hold the Christ-light for you
> In the night-times of your fear;
> I will hold my hand out to you,
> Speak the peace you long to hear.
>
> I will weep when you are weeping;
> When you laugh I'll laugh with you.
> I will share your joy and sorrow,
> 'Til we've seen this journey through.
>
> When we sing to God in heaven
> We shall find such harmony,
> Born of all we've known together
> Of Christ's love and agony.

'Servant Song', Richard Gillard

Do you think this is a suitable song for both marriage and ordination? List some reasons 'For' and 'Against'.

Living the Gospel

In this section of our work we will be learning:

◆ about the importance for a vision for life
◆ about the Christian vision in terms of the Kingdom of God and its challenge and influence in the world today.

What is a vision statement?

Most companies and organisations have a vision statement. A vision statement is a written statement of what a company should look like in a certain number of years. It should be based on the collective beliefs and values of that organisation.

A vision statement should both inspire and guide.

NB: 'Vision' and 'Mission' statement; the two words are generally used to mean the same thing.

Research

Collect vision statements from organisations in your local area.

Display and discuss your findings.

Write a vision statement for a new business or organisation of your choice.

Share these with each other.

Decide the five steps that would ensure this vision statement was put into practice.

Or: write your personal vision statement. You do not have to share this unless you wish.

Test your memory

What is your school's mission statement? What does it mean? Share as a class.

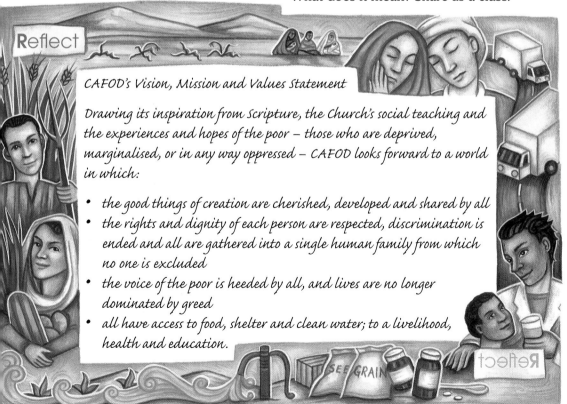

Reflect

CAFOD's Vision, Mission and Values Statement

Drawing its inspiration from Scripture, the Church's social teaching and the experiences and hopes of the poor – those who are deprived, marginalised, or in any way oppressed – CAFOD looks forward to a world in which:

• the good things of creation are cherished, developed and shared by all
• the rights and dignity of each person are respected, discrimination is ended and all are gathered into a single human family from which no one is excluded
• the voice of the poor is heeded by all, and lives are no longer dominated by greed
• all have access to food, shelter and clean water; to a livelihood, health and education.

One Gospel: many lives

The Gospel is the vision for all Christians. Each member of the Church is called to live in communion with Jesus, to respond to God's grace and to use the gifts of the Holy Spirit. Just as the four gospels proclaim the Good News of Jesus in their particular ways, so some individuals have been inspired by a particular Gospel value, for example, going apart to pray, feeding the hungry, compassion for the poor, teaching. In many cases these people became founders of religious orders, attracting other people to join them. The Church recognises the founders' personal visions as *charisms* for the whole Christian family and encourages those who want to dedicate their lives to living these visions.

charisms: gifts of the Holy Spirit; special ways God works through individuals

Three hundred years ago, *St John De La Salle* realised how important it was to organise schools for the street children of Reims, Paris and other cities in France. He founded schools as Christian communities and revolutionised education for ordinary people. He is known as the Patron Saint of teachers. This is part of the vision statement of the De La Salle Brothers: "We seek to devote our human resources to the service of those young people whose needs are greatest and who are unlikely to learn about the gospel unless we help them."

Fanny Margaret Taylor founded the Poor Servants of the Mother of God in 1866. This is part of their vision statement: "In response to God's incarnate love, we, the Poor Servants of the Mother of God, strive, like Mary, to be Christ-bearers to others, standing with them in their joys and insecurities. We seek to affirm the dignity and worth of all persons; and through our pastoral, healing and teaching ministries to respond to the demands of a particular time and place."

Father John Gailhac founded the Religious of the Sacred Heart of Mary in 1849. Part of their vision statement says: "We are called to be Community, to know and celebrate God's love for us and make that love known to others."

≡ Homework 🏛 ≡

Research a religious order or congregation near you or whose work interests you.

What is its title?

When was it formed and by whom?

What is its vision statement?

What is its work?

Jesus' Vision: The Kingdom of God

Jesus invited and challenged people to share a new vision. Matthew's gospel gives a collection of the teachings of Jesus in the Sermon on the Mount (Chapters 5–7). It begins with the Beatitudes (5:1–11).

'Beatitude' comes from the Latin *beati* meaning 'blessed by God'. Jesus invites people to live, not just by the letter of the law, but in a new spirit: the Beatitudes are a challenge to discover what true happiness is.

Today, it is in and through the Church that Jesus makes the same invitation and offers the same challenge. The Church is the community of all those who respond in faith.

The 'kingdom' the Beatitudes promise is not a place or a country. It is communion, meaning 'one in love', through Jesus with God the Father and the whole human family. The Church's vocation is to be this communion in every place and throughout history until it is complete and perfect in heaven. (Remember! Heaven is not a place. See 3A p. 73.)

Reflect

A vision statement is a launch pad for a great adventure.

It is the outcome of the desire to dream.

What would you include in your own vision statement?

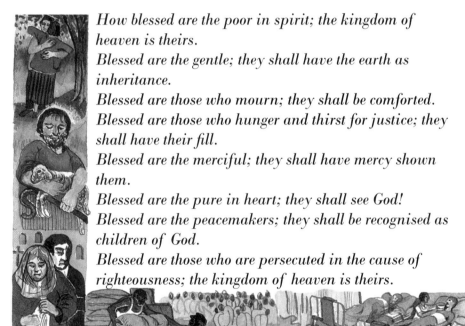

How blessed are the poor in spirit; the kingdom of heaven is theirs.
Blessed are the gentle; they shall have the earth as inheritance.
Blessed are those who mourn; they shall be comforted.
Blessed are those who hunger and thirst for justice; they shall have their fill.
Blessed are the merciful; they shall have mercy shown them.
Blessed are the pure in heart; they shall see God!
Blessed are the peacemakers; they shall be recognised as children of God.
Blessed are those who are persecuted in the cause of righteousness; the kingdom of heaven is theirs.

The Beatitudes are the values and vision of the Kingdom of God.

Work as a class

1. Discuss and identify:
   – the values expressed in the Beatitudes
   – some of the values the majority of people in our society hold today
   – similarities and differences between the two sets of values.

2. Name people who try to live out each of the Beatitudes. These could be individuals, groups or organisations. Use at least one of these sources: magazines, newspapers and career brochures.
   Display your answers in pictures and words.

3D Living the Gospel

Kingdom people

"You must be perfect ... just as your Father in heaven is perfect." (Matthew 5:48)

"Store up riches for yourself in heaven ... for your heart will always be where your riches are."
(Matthew 6:19–21)

"Do not judge others, so that God will not judge you."
(Matthew 7:1)

"You hypocrite! Take the log out of your own eye, and then you will be able to see clearly to take the speck out of your brother's eye." (Matthew 7:5)

The Golden Rule: "Do for others what you want them to do for you." (Matthew 7:12)

Discuss

What do these gospel texts say about God's call to each person?
What ideals for Christian living do you find in them?
What qualities would they help people to develop?
Which do you think are the most challenging?

Classwork

A. *Using one Beatitude for each day, write short thoughts and/or prayers for three days. Think about how you will bring out the vision and challenge of the Beatitude for today. Give each day a title.*

B. *Using examples from the work you have done, write an identikit for a Christian. Identify what age group you have in mind and what special challenges this would bring.*

C. *What questions would you want to put to Jesus about his teaching in the Sermon on the Mount? Write the dialogue you might have with him.*

Kingdom Vision

It helps now and then to step back and take the long view.

The Kingdom is not only beyond our efforts, it is beyond our vision.

We accomplish in our lifetime only a tiny fraction
*   of the magnificent enterprise which is God's work.*

Nothing we do is complete, which is another way of saying
*   that the Kingdom always lies beyond us.*

No statement says all that should be said.

No prayer fully expresses our faith.

No confession brings perfection.

No pastoral visit brings wholeness.

No programme accomplishes the Church's mission.

No set of goals includes everything.

This is what we are about:

We plant seeds that one day will grow.

We water the seeds already planted, knowing that the
*   future holds promise.*

We cannot do everything,
*   and there is a sense of liberation in realising that;*
*   this enables us to do something and do it very well.*

We may never see the end results, but that is the difference between the
*   Master Builder and the workers.*

We are workers, not the Master Builder,
*   ministers, not the Messiah.*

We are prophets of a future not our own.

Archbishop Oscar Romero

3D Living the Gospel

Class projects

Work in groups. Each group chooses A or B.

Plan your work so that at the end each group can make a presentation to the class and contribute to a display for the class or all Year 9.

You will need: one main message that you want people to remember; ways to help them remember this; ways to involve your audience.

> **The Magnificat**
>
> My heart praises the Lord;
> my soul is glad because of God my Saviour,
> for he has remembered me, his lowly
>   servant!
> From now on all people will call me happy,
> because of the great things the Mighty God
>   has done for me.
> His name is holy;
> from one generation to another he shows
>   mercy to those who honour him.
> He has stretched out his mighty arm
> and scattered the proud with all their
>   plans.
> He has brought down mighty kings from
>   their thrones, and lifted up the lowly.
> He has filled the hungry with good things,
> and sent the rich away with empty hands.
> He has kept the promise he made to our
>   ancestors,
> and has come to the help of his servant
>   Israel.
> He has remembered to show mercy to
>   Abraham
> and to all his descendants for ever!

1. Identify words and phrases that make this a song of praise.
2. What does the song say about the person praying it? Give reasons for your answer.
3. What does the song say about God's vision for the world?
4. How might this song of praise influence a Christian's lifestyle and behaviour? Give examples.

A. Mary's vision

Mary is a model disciple of Jesus. She said yes to God. She showed great faith and obedience when she said: "I am the handmaid of the Lord, let what you have said be done to me." (Luke 1:38)

Luke gives us a song of praise which sums up Mary's vision, concerns, attitudes and values. It is called the Magnificat (Luke 1:46–55). It is Mary's response to her cousin Elizabeth's greeting: "You are the most blessed of all women and blessed is the child you will bear!"

Extension

Use a church calendar or missal to find out the feasts the Church celebrates in honour of Mary. What does this say about her and her place in Catholic life?

B. A Vision of God: Icon of the Trinity

This is one of the most famous icons. It is the work of Andrei Rublev, an iconographer in Russia in the early fifteenth century.
An icon is a sacred image, a focus for prayer. Every detail of an icon is significant.
Use these notes to study the icon carefully.

Look up Genesis 18:1–15, from where the iconographer takes his inspiration.
Look at the figures.
What details has he used to evoke the story?

If you view this icon through a ring you will find that the figures make a perfect circle.
Begin your journey round the circle with the figure on the right.
Where is its look directed?
Next look at the central figure and see where its look is directed.
A circle is a symbol of time and love.
What is the iconographer saying about the Trinity?

Colours in icon painting are symbolic.
- blue for water
- green for life
- brown for earth, the world
- gold for majesty and authority
- shades of rose and violet for mystery.

Objects in icon painting are symbols.
A mountain for faith (Matthew 17:20).
A tree for creation and the cross.
A house for heaven, God's dwelling (John 14:5).

Use the colours and positions of the objects and the figures to decide which represents the Holy Spirit, the Son and the Father.

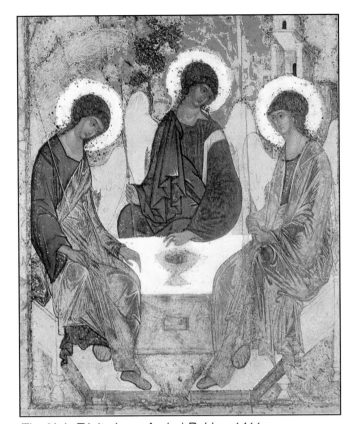

The Holy Trinity Icon, Andrei Rublev, 1411.

Look at the table around which they are gathered.
Who is the space at the front for?

Discuss

What is the icon inviting believers to do?
Has it anything to say to a non-believer?
Which of the following statements could describe the icon's message:
- the kingdom of heaven is the perfect love of Father, the Son and the Holy Spirit
- the kingdom of heaven is the work of the Father, the Son and the Holy Spirit
- the kingdom of heaven is the invitation to share the life and love of the Trinity.

Give reasons for your answers.

3D Living the Gospel

3

Glossary

Enter these words in your personal glossary with a brief explanation for each:

Sermon on the Mount
Magnificat
vision
charism

1. *Choose any religious order and explain their vision.*
2. *What are the Beatitudes?*
3. *What is the 'golden rule of life'?*
4. *What did Jesus say about judging others?*
5. *Select two quotes from the Magnificat that express Mary's faith in God.*

Reflect

Jesus said: "Anyone who hears these words of mine and obeys them is like a wise person who built their house on rock." (Matthew 7:24)

Living faith

O Lord, all the world belongs to you,
and you are always making all things new.
What is wrong you forgive,
and the new life you give
is what's turning the world upside down.

The world's only loving to its friends,
but you have brought us love that
never ends;
loving enemies too,
and this loving with you,
is what's turning the world upside down.

'Turning the world upside down',
Patrick Appleford

Dilemma

Is it impossible to love our enemies and do good to those who hate us?

Go further

Survey a variety of TV and magazine adverts. What evidence can you find of the influence of the Christian vision of the Kingdom of God? What does this say about how the Church is proclaiming the Gospel? Write a Comment Column for a Catholic or national newspaper.

Find this hymn if you do not already know it. What is its vision for Christian life?

Be creative

Design an icon that expresses what you believe is worth living for.